Mary Mulari's
Accessories
With
Style

Published by

krause publications
700 E. State St.
Iola, WI 54990-0001
Telephone 715-445-2214
www.krause.com

Please call or write for our free catalog. Our toll-free number to place an order or obtain a free catalog is 800-258-0929 or please use our regular business telephone 715-445-2214 for editorial comment and further information.

Photography by Don Hoffman, Rex McDonald Studio, Wadena, Minnesota
Illustrations by Mary Mulari

Library of Congress Catalog Number: 00-110060

ISBN: 0-87341-970-7

Printed in the United States of America

The following registered or trademarked products and companies appear:
All Night Media, Inc.®, Amazing Designs®, American Tourister, BabyLock, Bernina, Brother, C. M. Offray & Sons, Cactus Punch, Dan River Inc., Fiskars, FlashFelt by Kunin Felt™, Fray Check™, Heat n Bond® Lite Iron-On Adhesive, Hoffman Fabrics, Husqvarna Viking, Janome, Jean-a-ma-jig™, HTC's Craft Plus™, JHB International, June Tailor, Kunin Felt, Lycra®, Malden Mills, Michiko's Creations, Mini Fasturn®, Omnigrid®, P & B Fabrics, Pellon® Craft Fuse™, Pfaff, Polarfleece™, Prym Dritz, ReVisions, Sensuede™, Sewing with Nancy®, Singer, Sulky® KK2000™, Sulky of America, Therm O Web, Timber Lane Press, Timtex™, Totally Stable™, Ultrasuede®, Velcro®, Viking, Wrights®, YLI Jeans Thread.

Dedication

This book is dedicated to
Margaret W. Marvin
in appreciation of her friendship
and her support to libraries
and readers.

Acknowledgments

This book comes to you with my name on the cover and a great support group that deserves my thanks here at the beginning of the book. I appreciate very much the advice, help, information, and generosity extended to me.

Thanks to the following sewing machine companies, their educators, and staff: BabyLock, Bernina, Brother, Elan, Janome, Pfaff, Singer, and Viking.

Thanks to the following companies and their representatives for information and products: All Night Media, Dan River Inc., Fiskars, Hoffman Fabrics, JHB International, June Tailor, Kunin Felt, Malden Mills, C.M. Offray & Sons, P & B Fabrics, Pellon, Prym Dritz, ReVisions, Sulky of America, Therm O Web, Timber Lane Press, Wrights, and YLI Corporation.

My thanks to Nancy Zieman for her continued interest in my books and the opportunity to present the projects from this book as her guest on "Sewing with Nancy."

As before, my Project Review Personnel deserve thanks for their willingness to view the latest work and offer honest opinions: Sarah Koski, Nancy Harp, and Barry Mulari.

My friends and fellow Walkie-Talkies agreed to model for this book on a hot August day and didn't whine when I asked them to wear Polarfleece. Thanks to Naomi Dangelo, Lorraine Ekman, Nancy Harp, Helen Jones, Elsie Lehtinen, Joan Liimatta, Dorothy Ojala, and Helen Simonich. Thanks also to the Walkie-Talkies at the coffee table at Hank's Bar and Grill for modeling my gloves.

Thanks to the special and talented designers I'm pleased to present in this book: Rita Farro, Terri Johnson, Carolyn McCormick, Luveta Nickels, and Ann Sagawa.

For this book, special contributors deserve mention and my appreciation: Jeanne MacDonald and Karen Emerson for fabric and friendship; Joanne and Don Barstad of Don's True Value in Aurora, Minnesota; Linda Moser and her fabulous fabrics at Libertyville Sewing Center, Libertyville, Illinois; Mary Ann and Sheldon Porthan for golf accessory advice; and Marge Cornelius of the Mesaba Drug/Ben Franklin, Hoyt Lakes, Minnesota.

Very special thanks to Susan Keller for her critical reading of the manuscript, her review of its organization, and her excellent suggestions.

And finally, my thanks to my project editor Barbara Case for expertly guiding this book along the paths at Krause Publications.

Table of Contents

Introduction

What happened? The "Sweatshirt Queen" changed her topic!

Since 1982, I have been known for embellishments to sweatshirts and other plain clothing, so a book that features projects to wear and carry is a big change. Of course, after you make the projects in this book, you can still decorate them, and the designs and techniques in my other books will offer lots of ideas.

I haven't changed, however, in my emphasis on sewing ease, style, and sensibility. Like most of my decorating techniques, these projects are not difficult to make, yet they are distinctive, useful, and full of details that make them classy. You'll want to make them for yourself and also create unique gifts for others.

Some of the fabrics suggested and shown in this book may be exotic and different from your usual choices, so I challenge you to step out of your usual tracks. It'll be an adventure to sew with lace, tapestry, Ultrasuede, chalkboard fabric, vinyl, and even tablecloths, potholders, rugs, and window screen.

You can use my instructions and patterns as a jumping off point for your own designing ideas. Personalize the projects by choosing a different fabric, changing the sizes of a bag's handles or straps to make it more comfortable to carry, adding monograms, or embellishing with machine embroidery or couching. Choose a feature from one bag and sew it on a different one. I encourage you to use what I present here for your own enjoyment and to tailor accessories that are truly useful for you.

This is the first time one of my books has included pull-out pattern sheets in the back of the book. These tissue paper sheets are filled with many patterns for

Welcome to my home and my latest collection of sewing projects. I hope you will enjoy reading and using this book to create special accessories for your own use and for gifts too. In the photos of this book, you'll see scenes and pieces from my life here in Aurora, Minnesota: my walking group friends who cheerfully became models, my sister Sarah's quilts as backdrops, flowers from my garden, a rhubarb leaf set behind my garden journal, and more. Be sure to read the photo captions for details!

the projects in this book. If a piece is square or rectangular, the dimensions are listed in the project instructions and the pattern piece won't appear on the tissue pattern sheets. You can measure and mark these pieces directly on the fabric you've chosen, or make your own pattern pieces from paper if you plan to use the pattern several times.

Have a great time sewing my new collection of accessories. I would like to know how you've adapted my ideas and how others have responded to these projects when they received them as gifts. Please write to me at Box 87-K3, Aurora, MN 55705 or e-mail me: mary@marymulari.com.

Mary Mulari

Useful Supplies & Smart Techniques

$\mathcal{E}$ach of the projects in this book begins with a supply list to help you start off in an organized, efficient way. Most of the products will be commonly found in your sewing stash or in sewing stores or catalogs.

Collect your favorite trims and braids, buttons, tassels, and even a tape measure and hair accessories for embellishments and details on projects from this book. Buttons by JHB International. Trims, piping, and tassels by Wrights. Tape measure by Prym Dritz.

Supplies

Several products and tools are mentioned frequently and you'll want to have them handy. I came to rely on invisible nylon threads, Ultrasuede pieces and scraps, pinking shears, a 3" x 18" ruler, crisp interfacing, and Velcro as I designed and sewed for this book.

INVISIBLE NYLON THREAD

Clear and smoke varieties of nylon thread by YLI.

This thread comes in two "colors" - clear and smoke. The clear variety looks like very fine fishing line, and when sewn it blends well with light and medium colors. On printed fabrics, it blends in so well you can hardly see the seamline. The smoke variety blends best with dark fabrics. Have both on hand for the projects in this book. In addition, fill a bobbin with each color. These threads are soft, but very strong. Instead of changing thread colors often, you can use the same clear thread through the entire project.

ULTRASUEDE (OR SENSUEDE)

Small pieces of Ultrasuede in a variety of colors will be a handy resource in your sewing room. Assortment by Michiko's Creations.

Pieces and scraps of Ultrasuede are very versatile. They can work as strong handles for bags, neat no-fray covers for bag handle ends, and classy ties for zipper pulls. I believe every sewing artist needs an Ultrasuede collection. Once you begin using it, I know you'll love it and want to use more. Just remember to cover it with a press cloth before you iron it. (Another brand name of this fabric is Sensuede. See the Resources, page 96, for sources of these wonderful machine washable and dryable fabrics.)

PINKING SHEARS

The instructions for so many of the projects will direct you to trim and clip seam allowances. You can do it in two steps with standard scissors, but by trimming with pinking shears, you'll save time doing both steps at once. Another option is to use a rotary cutter with a pinking blade.

3"x 18" RULER

This ruler proved to be most helpful when making the accessories in this book. Many of the bag handles are 3" wide so using this ruler makes them very quick to cut with a rotary cutter on a mat or rule off to cut with scissors.

CRISP INTERFACING

To make accessories that are durable and substantial, such as bags for toting heavy things, crisp interfacing is a key ingredient. Even everyday purses and tote bags will wear better if a layer of crisp interfacing is fused onto light or medium-weight fabric before sewing;

Three types of interfacing used for the projects in this book: Timtex for hat brims, Pellon's Craft Fuse for crisp interfacing, and HTC's Craft Plus for crisp interfacing with a thin layer of quilt batting.

they become the sturdy fabrics required for many projects. Varieties I recommend are Craft Fuse by Pellon (nonwoven interfacing with fusible backing) and Crafts Plus by HTC, a low-loft nonwoven fusible fabric backing. For soft and flexible hat brims and even firmer support for bags, use Timtex interfacing.

VELCRO

Velcro, showing both the hook and loop sides that hold together for a great accessory closure.

What would we do without this space-age invention? Velcro is easy to attach and makes a durable, sensible fastener. I like to have many colors on hand so there's a good chance to blend the Velcro color with my project. Strips of 3/4" width are easy to find and are used throughout this book. Sometimes I cut the strip in half down the middle to make it narrower.

Techniques

Back in the '50s when I was in the Loon Lake 4-H Club sewing program, I learned some good rules that continue to make a difference in my sewing. This is the time to share them with you, or remind you of some habits you've already acquired while sewing.

1. Press every seam you sew to smooth the seamline and embed the thread into the fabric. Then when you open the seam or turn the fabric right side out, you'll press the seamline again. These steps will help you create professional looking accessories, as well as garments.

2. When sewing a seam and leaving an opening to turn the fabric right side out, sew down from the fabric edges to the seam allowance, then turn the fabric to continue the seam. Do the same on the other end of the stitching. (Fig. 1) This makes a neater opening that's less likely to fray and easy to press flat.

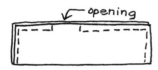

Fig. 1

3. Pay attention to the size of the sewing machine needle and the length of time you've used it. Change needles often, and make sure they're the appropriate size for the fabrics you're sewing. Many of the bags use several layers of heavy fabrics, so you'll need to use a correctly sized needle that won't break when you sew through thick layers and corners. In cases where a special needle size is required, the instructions indicate what size to use. Discard the used needles so you won't be confused or tempted to use them again.

4. One sign of style in any accessory or garment is very subtle but very important: thread color. Take the time to match the color of the thread to the fabric. Unless you want to topstitch with a high contrast color thread, the match of the thread to the fabric speaks to the care you take with your sewing and your intention to create classy projects.

5. Many instructions in this book encourage you to use either a second seam or reinforced stitches. Both serve to strengthen seamlines for the real-life use of bags and other accessories. Many sewing machine reinforced stitches are indicated with similar drawings and named triple straight stitch or a similar title. (Fig. 2) Experiment with them and you'll notice that the stitching line is more noticeable than a regular straight stitch. You might want to use a reinforced stitch as a topstitching detail also.

Fig. 2

6. To shape many of the bags in this book, you will stitch a straight seam across the corner inside the bag. Meet the side seam to the bottom center seam to form a triangle. Sew across the triangle on a straight line. (Fig. 3)

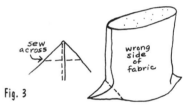

Fig. 3

Do this on each side of the bag. A 1" line will form a narrower bottom to the bag than a 4" line. (Fig. 4) The length of the line will be indicated in each project.

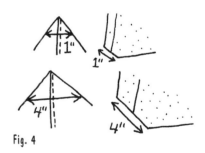

Fig. 4

Be prepared to see many uses for zippers in this book. There's no need to let zippers scare you away, especially after you learn a very easy way to sew them onto bags and pockets. Turn to the next page to read about Exposed Zippers and Anything Pockets and Bags.

Exposed Zippers & Anything Pockets and Bags

any times I hear the guests at my seminars saying, "I'll sew anything as long as it doesn't have a zipper." The time has come to develop a new attitude about zipper sewing. It can be easy, as you'll see with the Exposed Method of zipper application which I developed first for my book *Travel Gear and Gifts to Make*.

1. Select a piece of fabric and a nylon zipper longer than the fabric is wide. (Fig. 1)

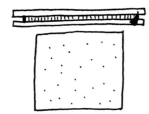

Fig. 1

Use the very quick-and-easy exposed zipper method and fabric of your choice to make a handy bag for cosmetics, school supplies, crochet hooks, or just about ANYTHING!

You can use zippers of the same length as the fabric, but it's much easier to have zippers that are too long. After sewing the zipper, you'll cut off the ends and easily avoid sewing into the metal pieces at the zipper ends.

Pin the zipper 1" from the top edge of the piece of fabric, meeting the wrong side of the zipper to the right side of the fabric. (Fig. 2)

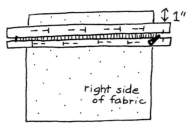

Fig. 2

2. Sew along the outer edge of the zipper sides and across the short ends. You may not need to put on the zipper foot to do this. Adjust the sewing machine needle, if you can, to a left-needle position. Sew back and forth across the short ends, and on the end where the zipper head is located, make sure it is pulled open and inside the seamline across the zipper. (Fig. 3)

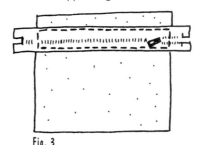

Fig. 3

To make the zipper very secure, especially if the fabric frays easily, sew a second line around the zipper, sewing closer to the zipper teeth. (Fig. 4)

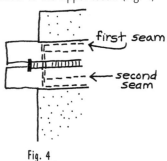

Fig. 4

3. Trim away the excess length of the zipper beyond the stitching lines on both ends of the zipper. On the back of the fabric, cut away the fabric over the zipper teeth. (Fig. 5) Now you have a zipper opening in the piece of fabric. Wasn't that easy?

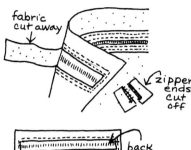

Fig. 5

4. To cover part of the zipper sides, you can sew on bias tape, decorative braid, or other trim. This is not required, but you'll see it done on several zippers in the book, and you may like to add this decorative detail on your projects also. (Fig. 6)

Fig. 6

5. To turn this piece of fabric into an Anything Pocket that you could sew onto a lining of a tote bag, a purse, or garment, turn under and press the four sides of the piece of fabric. (Fig. 7)

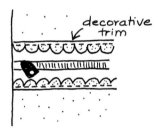

Fig. 7

Pin the pocket onto the lining or backing of a bag of your choice and sew around the edges.

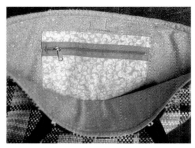

An Anything Pocket adds a secure storage place for keys or money inside the Shopping Tote (see page 24 for the tote instructions).

6. For an Anything Bag, cut another piece of fabric the same size as the fabric with the zipper. (Fig. 8)

Fig. 8

Open the zipper a short way and pin the two fabrics with right sides together. Sew around the four sides, sewing a double or reinforced seam if you want the bag to be extra strong. Press and trim the seam allowances, clipping at the corners. (Fig. 9)

Fig. 9

Turn the bag right side out through the zipper opening. Press the seamlines again. You now have a wonderful bag to store anything you want. That's why we call them Anything Bags

Anything Bags can be any shape and size.

The photo below shows a sampling of the bags I've made. They're very useful and can be made in any size and shape. Several of the projects in the book use this basic Anything Bag method and you'll be referred to these pages for the instructions.

Anything Bags made from a variety of fabrics, even the pocket from an old pair of jeans. Some of the zippers have added trim on the sides, and they all have a pull tied to the zipper head to make it easy to open and close the zipper.

Use the Anything Bag method to make this stylish portfolio from tapestry fabric. Cut two pieces of fabric 16-1/2" wide x 12" high. The handle is a 14" piece of webbing sewn to the top seam of the bag.

Totes & Purses

Separating-Zipper Tote

Add the feature of a separating zipper to the sides of a tote bag for both function and decoration. Closed, the zipper provides a convenient, compact way to store the tote, and opened, the zipper serves as seamline trim, especially if the zipper color contrasts with the tote fabric.

The sides of this tote bag have a detail for both style and function: a separating zipper. Open the zipper to fill and carry the tote bag, then close it to store the tote. The aqua tote has a matching color zipper which blends with the tote. The red zipper on the black tote creates more noticeable trim.

Supply List:

1/2 yd. fabric for tote (I used cordura nylon & recommend any sturdy fabric 45" wide or wider)

16" separating zipper

1 yd. nylon webbing for handles

7" or shorter zipper for pocket inside bag lining

Optional:
   1/2 yd. fabric for tote lining

1. Cut two pieces of fabric 16" wide and 18-1/2" long. Also cut two lining pieces the same size if you plan to line the bag.

2. Sew the 16" bottom edges together with a 1/2" seam allowance, with the right sides of the fabric facing. Make sure to reinforce the stitching by sewing twice, using a reinforced stitch, or sewing a double seam. Sew appliques or extra outer pockets to the tote at this time.

3. Pin and sew each side of the separating zipper to the sides of the same fabric piece, placing the bottom edge of the zipper at the bottom seamline. Fold back the excess zipper tape at the top edge. (Fig. 1)

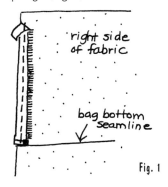

right side of fabric

bag bottom seamline

Fig. 1

4. Turn the bag wrong side out by bringing the other half of the tote over the zipper side, meeting the right sides of the tote fabric. Pin the edges together on both sides. Sew the sides together by following the first seamline that attached the zipper to the fabric. Continue stitching all the way to the top of the tote. (Fig. 2)

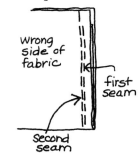

Wrong side of fabric

first seam

Fig. 2   Second seam

5. Trim and clip the seam allowances at the bottom corners of the tote.

6. This is the time to line the bag. Sew an Anything Pocket to the bag lining before assembling it. Follow the instruc-

tions on page 8 for making the pocket. Position and sew the pocket 4" down from the top edge of one of the lining fabrics. (Fig. 3)

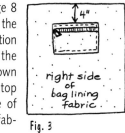

4"

right side of bag lining fabric.

Fig. 3

7. Sew the lining pieces together (right sides facing) on the sides and bottom. Trim and press the seams. Slide the lining into the tote with the right side of the lining inside. Match the lining to the bag at the side seams and pin it in place. You may wish to trim away some of the fabric from the top edge of the lining to avoid extra bulk when turning under the tote's top edges.

8. Turn under 1/4" and press the top edge of the tote fabric. Then turn under and press the fabric once more to line up with the top edge of the zipper. This forms the facing on the top inside edge of the bag. (Fig. 4)

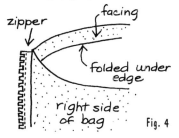

facing

zipper

folded under edge

right side of bag   Fig. 4

9. Now it's time to make the tote handles, each of which is 18" long. Make the handles from the tote fabric by cutting a 3" x 18" piece of fabric for each handle, sewing right sides together as illustrated and turning right side out through the opening. (Fig. 5)

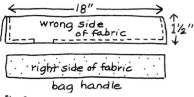

18"

wrong side of fabric   1½"

right side of fabric
bag handle

Fig. 5

I used nylon webbing for the tote handles and added lining fabric as trim. Cut 18" strips of lining fabric twice as wide as the webbing. Sew a 1/4" seam to attach one edge of the webbing to the right side of the fabric. Bring the

second long edge of the fabric to the opposite side of the webbing and sew a 1/4" seam. (Fig. 6) Turn the webbing handles right side out.

right side of fabric

right side of fabric

nylon webbing

nylon webbing

Fig. 6

10. Pin each handle to the inside facing of the top of the bag, placing each end 4" from the side seams. Turn under and pin the fabric edges at the bottom of each webbing handle. Sew each handle end to the facing only. (Fig. 7)

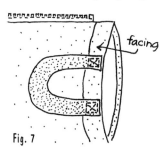

facing

Fig. 7

11. Pin the inside facing in place, placing the pins on the outside of the tote. Sew the facing in place from the right side of the tote. Begin stitching at the edge of one side of the zipper and stop stitching at the edge on the opposite side. Do not sew over the zipper teeth. (Fig. 8)

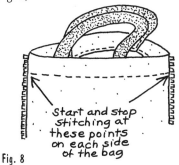

Start and stop stitching at these points on each side of the tote

Fig. 8

Tuck the handles inside the tote and zip the sides together.

The eye-catching zipper detail of this tote bag adds the useful feature of easy and compact storage.

Girlfriends' Beach Tote

Sometimes it's hard to find mesh fabric for making bags, so I chose lace fabric instead. Like mesh, it has openings to air out the bag's contents, and it's a perfect choice for a woman... maybe your girlfriend who'd appreciate the features of this bag for her trips to the beach or the gym. She can store her shoes or her lunch in the bottom zippered section and carry a towel and clothing in the top lace section.

Collect your beach wear and supplies in this lace-sided bag with a separate bottom compartment. Drawstrings pull the top casing together and a shoulder strap on the back of the bag makes it easy to carry. It's perfect for everything you need to carry for a girlfriends' day at the beach.

Supply List:

1 yd. lace fabric, 45" wide or wider

1/2 yd. canvas or sturdy fabric for bottom section

24" or 26" zipper

4" x 45" lighter weight fabric strip for top drawstring casing

3 yds. cording for drawstrings

1 yd. crisp interfacing

1/8 yd. tear-away stabilizer

Optional:

10" x 15" piece of vinyl or waterproof nylon

22" webbing for shoulder strap

1. On the tissue pattern sheets, locate the piece for the Girlfriend's Beach Tote base. Cut two from canvas fabric and a third from vinyl or nylon for a waterproof bottom of the lace section of the bag. (A waterproof layer will prevent wet swimwear and towels from soaking through the top of the zippered bottom section.)

2. For the side wall of the bottom section of the bag, cut a 7"-wide strip of canvas fabric to the exact length of the zipper. Cut a second 7"-wide canvas strip so the two strips equal 41" in length. For example, I used a 26" zipper and cut the main 7" strip to that length. Then I cut a second strip 15" long. (Fig. 1)

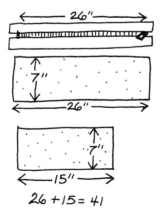

Fig. 1

Interface all four pieces of the fabric: both 7" strips and the two base shapes.

3. Mark a solid line on the right side of the zipper-length strip, 1-1/4" down from the top edge. (Fig. 2)

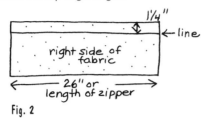

Fig. 2

Pin the zipper right side up to the fabric strip, lining up the upper edge of the zipper with the line you drew. Sew the zipper to the fabric. Add a second row of stitching to secure the zipper.

For a lacy edge to the zipper, sew a decorative stitch with YLI Jeans thread, using a topstitching (size 100) needle. I chose thread to match the zipper color. Practice on scraps of the fabric with interfacing on the back. Select a decorative stitch and sew an inch or so to see what it looks like with thicker thread. Sew slowly. Once you've selected the stitch you like, sew along each long edge of the zipper. The interfacing will serve as a stabilizer.

Add lace-like edging to the zipper by stitching with YLI Jeans thread on the sides of the exposed zipper.

4. Sew the second 7" strip to each end of the zipper piece, right sides together, sewing over the zipper ends and using a 1/2" seam allowance. Sew slowly and carefully over the zipper ends to prevent breaking the needle. Mark the quarter portions on one of the canvas bag base pieces and on the non-zipper edge of the circle of fabric with the zipper. Match and pin the marks together with the right sides of the fabric together. (Fig. 3)

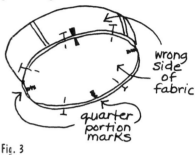

Fig. 3

Sew the bag base to the side section, reinforcing the stitches or sewing around twice. You may want to clean-finish all the bag edges by serging or zigzag stitching the seam allowances.

5. Sew the top of the zippered bag section to the other base. Meet the wrong side of the second interfaced base fabric to the inside of the zippered section, matching quarter portion lines again. If you plan to add the waterproof layer of vinyl or nylon, also pin it on at this time with the wrong side facing the right side of the interfaced base layer. Sew both the layers to the zippered section. (Fig. 4)

Fig. 4

6. Prepare the top lace section of the bag by cutting two pieces of lace 17" x 41". With the two layers together, sew the lace into a circle, stitching along the 17" sides with the right sides of the lace together. (Fig. 5)

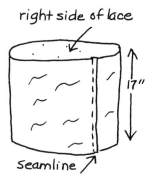

right side of lace

17"

Seamline

Fig. 5

7. Cut a 4" x 41" strip of fabric for the casing at the top of the lace section. I suggest cotton or a lightweight nylon for this casing to help it draw up more easily and form a tight closure. Sew the strip into a circle by meeting the 4" ends, right sides together. Turn under and press 1/4" on each long edge of the circle, then press the band in half with the fabric right side out. With the seamline of the casing at the center back, fold and mark the other three quarter portions. (Fig. 6)

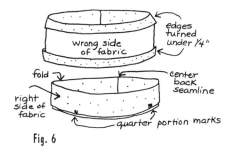

edges turned under 1/4"

wrong side of fabric

fold

center back seamline

right side of fabric

quarter portion marks

Fig. 6

8. Stitch a 1/2"-long buttonhole through the front layer of the casing on each of the two side marks (not on the center front mark), keeping the 1/4"

seam allowances out of the way. Use a small piece of stabilizer under each buttonhole. (Fig. 7)

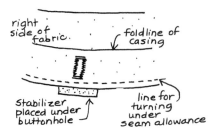

right side of fabric.

foldline of casing

Stabilizer placed under buttonhole

line for turning under seam allowance

Fig. 7

Pin the casing to the top of the lace, inserting the lace about 1/2" into the casing and meeting the back seamlines of the lace and the casing. Also insert one end of the shoulder strap at the seamline. Sew around the folded over edges of the casing. (Fig. 8)

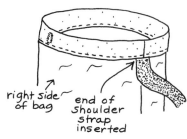

right side of bag

end of shoulder strap inserted

Fig. 8

9. Turn the lace section wrong side out and pin its bottom edge to the top edge of the zippered section. Match the lace seamline with the center of the fabric section without the zipper. Sew around, again with reinforced stitches or a second seam. (Fig. 9)

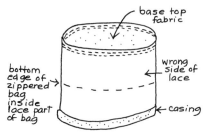

base top fabric

bottom edge of zippered bag inside lace part of bag

wrong side of lace

casing

Fig. 9

10. Sew the loose end of the shoulder strap to the bottom edge of the zippered section. To prevent the webbing from raveling, treat it first with Fray Check or other fray stopping liquid, or zigzag back and forth while attaching the strap. (Fig. 10)

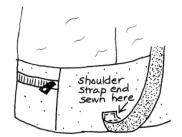

shoulder strap end sewn here

Fig. 10

11. Cut the three yards of cording in half. Lace one piece through the casing in one of the buttonholes and out the same buttonhole. Lace the second piece in and out of the opposite buttonhole. Knot the cords and pull together to close the top of the bag. (Fig. 11)

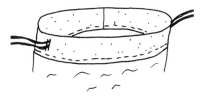

Fig. 11

Have a great time with your girlfriends and this handy bag on your next trip to the beach, the pool, or aerobics class.

Multi-Task Tote

Talk about a bag perfect for the busy woman! This tote has so many features to appreciate: side pockets (one perfect for a water bottle and the other with a zipper opening), a large open pocket trimmed with machine embroidery and a monogram, a fabric frame with interchangeable inserts (including chalkboard fabric for list making), a unique handle system, and a top extension to add more to the bag and hold it all in safely. If you don't want to use all these ideas, select the features just right for your own multi-task tote.

Carry what you need for all your tasks in this versatile bag. The front features a frame for a piece of chalkboard fabric or other fabric artwork, all attached with Velcro and changeable inside the frame. As I wrote the grocery list for the bag, I thought of writing "milk, bread, eggs," but decided on fun foods instead! Notice the side pocket for a water bottle and the unique handles on the top edge of the tote. Tote fabric by Dan River.

Store a pair of glasses or often-needed supplies in the large pocket on the back of the Multi-Task Tote. Featured on this pocket are a large embroidery created on a Husqvarna Viking Designer 1 sewing machine and an applique monogram. Other details of this tote are the side zipper pocket and the extension for the bag, which zips closed when extended from the top of the bag. Carry the bag over your shoulder or as a backpack.

Supply List:
1 yd. sturdy fabric, 45" wide
1/2 yd. lining fabric
Optional:
   7" zipper for side pocket
   20" zipper for bag top extension
   small piece of paper-backed fusible web
   6" strip Velcro, 3/4" wide
   cellophane tape, 1/2" wide

1. Cut the following pieces from bag fabric:
   2 pieces 14" x 15" for the back and front
   2 pieces 7" x 22" for the bag sides and bottom

2. Cut the following pieces for the optional features:
   8" square for the window frame
   8" square from the lining fabric
   2 pieces 6" x 21" for the bag top extension

   9" x 10" piece for the water bottle side pocket
   12" x 10" fabric piece for the flat, open pocket on the bag front
   2 pieces 3" x 30" for the bag straps
   3" x 11" fabric strip for the handle.

3. Prepare each side of the tote with its feature before assembling the tote bag. (Assembling instructions continue with Step 7.) On the bag back, sew the large flat pocket. I turned under and pressed the edges of a machine embroidery sample, added the monogram (see page 93), and turned my stitching experiment into a pocket. (Fig. 1)

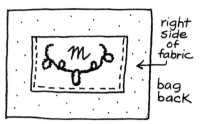

Fig. 1

4. The bag front features a **fabric frame** with changeable pictures, including machine embroideries, a piece of chalkboard fabric, or an interesting piece of printed fabric. The frame is made from the 8" square of bag and lining fabric. With the right sides of the fabric together, draw lines 1-1/2" from each edge to make a square in the center. Sew the two fabrics together along the lines. (Fig. 2)

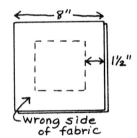

Fig. 2

Trim both fabrics from the center, trim the seam allowances, and clip to the corners. (Fig. 3)

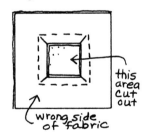

Fig. 3

With the lining side up, turn the lining fabric to the back through the opening and press the opening. Trim away 1/2" from the outer edges of the lining fabric and use pieces of paper-backed fusible web to secure the lining to the back of the frame. Turn under

1/4" and press the outside edges of the right side of the frame. (Fig. 4)

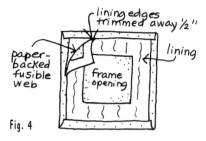

Fig. 4

Mark a 6" square on the front of the tote bag piece. (Fig. 5)

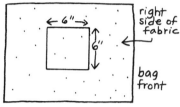

Fig. 5

Cut four 2" long x 3/8" wide strips of the hook (rough) side of Velcro and sew on the center line of each side of the square. (Fig. 6)

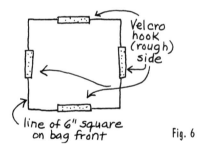

Fig. 6

Position and pin the frame to the bag, making sure all four pieces of Velcro are hidden under the frame. Sew the outside edge of the frame to the bag. (Fig. 7)

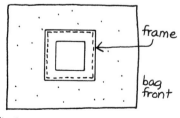

Fig. 7

Prepare pieces of "art" for the center of the frame by cutting 6" squares,

fusing interfacing to the back to stabilize the fabric, and sewing small pieces of the loop (soft) side of Velcro to the center of each edge. (Fig. 8)

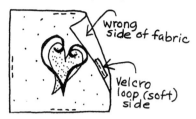

Fig. 8

Insert the art pieces inside the frame and match up the Velcro pieces to hold the art in place. Store the interchangeable pictures in the flat pocket on the other side of the bag.

5. For the **bag side with the zipper pocket**, mark a center line on the right side of one of the side pieces. Place a strip of 1/2"-wide cellophane tape 3" from the top edge of the bag side and extending on the line for the length of the zipper you plan to use. (Fig. 9)

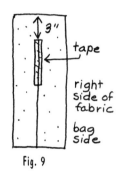

Fig. 9

With a short stitch length on the sewing machine, sew around the four sides of the tape. Remove the tape and cut up the center of the fabric within the stitching lines, cutting carefully to the corners. Turn under the cut edges to the edges of the seamlines and press. (Fig. 10)

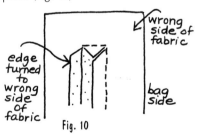

Fig. 10

Fit the zipper inside the opening so it faces out of the opening, pin, and stitch it in place. Cut a piece of lining fabric for the back of the zipper pocket. I cut mine

7" x 12". Turn under (toward the wrong side of the lining) or serge the 7" edges and pin and sew the piece to the back of the side fabric. This will form the pocket behind the zipper opening on the outside of the bag. (Fig. 11)

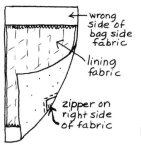

Fig. 11

6. To form the **water bottle pocket**, serge or turn under, then press and sew one 9" edge of the pocket fabric. Sew a gathering stitch on the opposite 9" edge. Draw a line across the bag side 12" from the top edge. Pull the gathering threads and fit the gathered edge, right side of the pocket to the right side of the bag, along the line. Pin and sew in place, making sure to reinforce this seam. (Fig. 12)

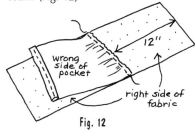

Fig. 12

Turn the pocket up and sew the sides to the bag sides.

7. Sew the center bottom edges of the bag sides together and reinforce the seam. This long strip forms the bag sides and bottom, with the seam at the bottom center. Pin and sew the bag fronts to the bag sides and bottom with the right sides of the fabric together, using a 1/2" seam allowance. (Fig. 13)

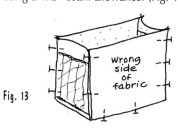

Fig. 13

Reinforce the seams. Serge or zigzag seam allowances to neaten the edges and prevent fraying.

8. Add the **bag top extension** at this time. Sew the 20" zipper to the 21" edges of the extension fabrics. Sew the side seams to make a circle. (Fig. 14)

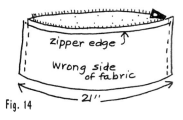

Fig. 14

Pin the raw edges of the extension to the top edge of the tote bag with the right sides of the fabric facing. Sew with a 1/4" seam, trim the seam allowance, press, and turn the extension inside the bag. Press again and sew on the right side of the bag 1/4" from the edge. (Fig. 15)

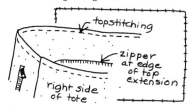

Fig. 15

The extension will be unzipped inside the bag until you want to load the bag and close the top. Then pull the extensions out and over the bag opening and zip it closed.

9. Make easy **handles and straps** for this tote by pressing under 1/4" on one long edge of each strap and handle piece. On the other edge, turn under 1" and press. Fold the 1/4" fold over and press again to form a 1" strap. (Fig. 16)

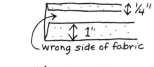

Fig. 16

Sew down the center and your strap is ready without having to turn anything right side out.

10. On the bag front with the frame, mark the center at the top edge and pin the two long strap pieces 2" from the top. Sew along the end of each strap and 1" up along each strap edge to anchor the straps to the bag, remembering to pull out the bag top extension before sewing! Cut a piece of bag fabric 3-1/2" x 2" to cover the strap ends. Turn under and press the four edges and sew the piece over the strap ends. (Fig. 17)

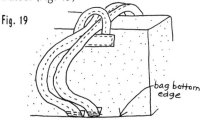

Fig. 17

Sew the bag handle to the bag back. Place the ends 2" down from the bag's top edge and centered 2" apart. Sew the ends to the bag. Cut a piece of fabric 2" x 6", turn under and press the edges, and sew the piece over the ends of the handle. (Fig. 18)

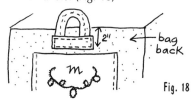

Fig. 18

11. Pass the two long straps through the handle and sew the ends to the bottom edge of the bag back, as illustrated. (Fig. 19)

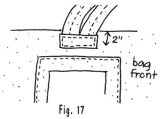

Fig. 19

Options:
* Line the bag or add an extra layer of fabric to the bottom to strengthen it.
* Consider this bag as a possible laptop computer carrier. With the bag top extension to close the tote bag and hide its contents, no one will know what you're carrying.

Back Strap Tote

Carry this bag over your shoulder or as a backpack with the zippered strap option. You'll find a handy front pocket for your sunglasses and the bag's zipper opening on the back is against your body so no one else has access to it. This makes more sense to me than the backpacks with exposed openings.

The separating zipper on the handle of this Back Strap Tote can be opened to wear the bag as a backpack, or closed for a single handle. On the front of the tote is a handy pocket. On the back (and inaccessible to thieves when you wear or carry the bag) is the main zipper opening to the bag.

The back of this variation of the Back Strap Tote shows the zipper opening and a solid purse handle without a separating zipper. Sarah's patchwork quilt makes a nice background to show off this Ultrasuede bag.

Supply List:

1 yd. sturdy fabric, 45" wide or wider
9" to 12" zipper
22" separating zipper for backpack strap that splits in two
7" square of lighter weight fabric for pocket lining
cellophane tape, 1/2" wide

Optional:
26" piping for pocket edges
fusible spray

1. Cut the bag fabric 13" x 34". On the tissue pattern sheets, locate the piece for the Back Strap Tote pocket and cut one pocket from the bag fabric and one from the lining fabric.

2. First you'll sew in the zipper opening on the back side of the bag. Draw a center line on one side of the right side of the bag piece. This will be the line for placing the zipper. Place 1/2"-wide tape on the centerline, starting 3" from the bag's top edge and extending to the end of the zipper. (Fig. 1)

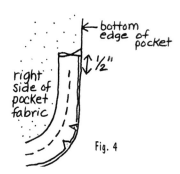

Fig. 1

On fabrics that fray, such as the tapestry bag shown, sew along all four sides of the tape, remove the tape, and cut a straight line in the center with diagonal cuts to each corner. (Fig. 2)

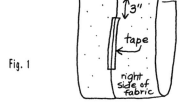

Fig. 2

Turn under and press the cut edges to make a neat rectangular opening in the fabric. On Ultrasuede and other non-fray fabrics, simply cut carefully around all four sides of the tape to remove the fabric.

Place the zipper on the wrong side of the fabric so it shows through the opening, pin carefully, and sew to secure it. I prefer to sew two seams a little distance apart for a better hold. (Fig. 3)

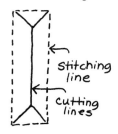

Fig. 3

3. Make the pocket for the front side of the bag. Piping adds a touch of style to the pocket and it's easy to sew on because all the corners of the pocket are rounded. Use a machine presser foot with a wide groove beneath to allow for the piping to pass under more smoothly. Also move the needle position to create a seam that holds the cord inside the piping. Start sewing 1/2" from the end of the piping. At the corners, clip the piping seam allowance so it curves around more easily. (Fig. 4)

Fig. 4

Stop sewing 1" from the end of the piping and cut the piping 1/2" longer than needed. Pull out and cut off 1/2" of the cord inside. Wrap the fabric around the beginning of the piping, turning it under at the edge, and stitch across for a neat joining. (Fig. 5)

Fig. 5

Place and pin the pocket lining to the pocket, with right sides meeting, and the piping in between. Sew around the pocket, stitching along the seamline that attached the piping. Leave a small opening along one of the sides. Trim the seam allowance and turn right side out through the opening. Press from the lining side. Remember to use a press cloth with Ultrasuede. Position the pocket centered on the bag front and 7" below the bag's top edge. Use a reinforced seam to sew it on the bag front. (Fig. 6)

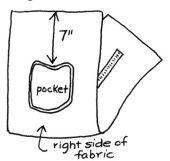

Fig. 6

4. Fold the bag in half, wrong sides out. Mark the bottom foldline on each side of the bag. Fold the mark up and inside the bag 2". (Fig. 7)

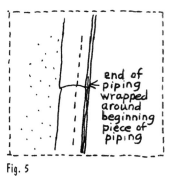

Fig. 7

This pleat will give form to the bag. Pin and sew both sides using a 1/2" seam allowance. Turn the bag right side out.

5. Fold and pleat the bag's top opening. Bring the seamlines together inside the bag and pin the folds in place. (Fig. 8)

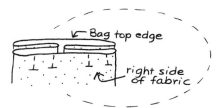

Fig. 8

Sew across the top, sewing 3/4" from the top edge to catch all folded edges and inside corners. Trim the seam allowance after determining that all pleats and edges are within the seamline.

6. Cut a piece of fabric 2-1/2" x 14". Fold it in half with right sides together and sew across the 2-1/2" ends to make a circle. Press the seam and slide the circle over the end of the bag, with right sides together. (Fig. 9)

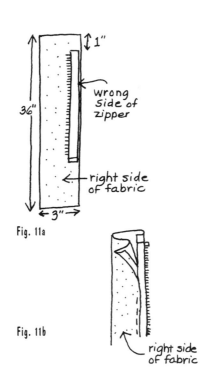

Fig. 11a

Fig. 9

Position the seamline to line up with the zipper. Sew across the bag top, again making sure to catch all the corners and edges of the folds. Bring the fabric up so that the right side shows. Turn under 1/2" and press the top edge. (Fig. 10)

Fig. 11b

For the Ultrasuede bag with a solid back strap and no zipper, cut a 4" x 36" strip of Ultrasuede. Draw a line on the wrong side in the center. Spray the back of the Ultrasuede strip with fusible spray. Bring one edge up to the line and pat it in place. Fold the opposite side down over the other edge. Sew to secure. (Fig. 12)

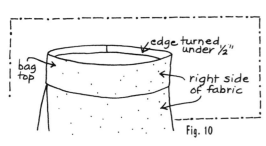

Fig. 10

7. For the bag strap with the separating zipper, cut two strips of fabric 3" x 36". Place and sew the wrong side of one half of the zipper 1" from the top and along one edge of the right side of one of the fabric strips. (Fig. 11a) Then press the opposite edge of the fabric strip under 1/4" and bring the fold to the zipper edge. Press and pin. Sew this edge in place on the right side of the zipper. (Fig. 11b) Attach the fabric to the other side of the zipper in the same way.

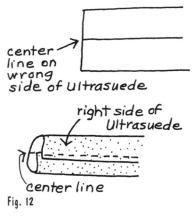

Fig. 12

8. Pin the bag handles to the bag and try it on to determine the correct length. Insert the top of the handle into the pressed under edge of the bag top. (Fig. 13)

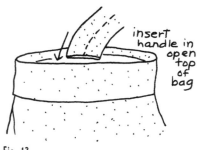

Fig. 13

Sew across with reinforced stitches to make the handle strong and secure. Sew the bottom edge of the handle to the bottom edge of the bag so it is centered with the line of the zipper.

Don't forget to add zipper pulls to make it easier to open the zippers on this bag.

Special Occasion Purses

Use the basic Anything Bag instructions on pages 8-9 to construct the purses featured here. You can see that even though the method of making them is simple, the results can be as elegant and formal as any special event might require.

Get ready for a night at the opera, the prom, or any dress-up occasion with one of these purses. On the left, the tapestry bag features a trimmed zipper and a short self-fabric handle. I added one of my jewelry pins to decorate the front. The black and purple bag in the center is made from iridescent FlashFelt by Kunin Felt. The handle is braided satin cords, and the top flap of the purse is a perfect place to add another of my favorite pins. The third bag is made from black velour with a coordinating black and purple print for the top flap. A black tassel from Wrights completes the simple but elegant style of the bag.

Elegant Black Purse

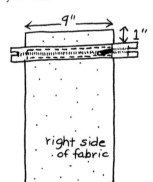

1. Refer to the Anything Bag instructions on page 8. Cut a piece of fabric 9" x 16". Add interfacing to the fabric to make it crisper and/or add lining fabric. Sew the zipper, right side up, to the right side of the purse fabric 1" down from one 9" end. (Fig. 1) Cut the fabric away behind the zipper. Add decorative trim over the edges of the zipper if you wish.

Fig. 1

2. On the tissue pattern sheets, locate the piece for the Special Occasion Purse Top Flap and cut two from fabric. Sew the right sides of the two top flap pieces together with a 1/4" seam allowance, leaving the top (straight)

edge open. For an extra touch of elegance, I added a black tassel which I sewed into the seam and reinforced the stitching. (Fig. 2)

Fig. 2

Trim the seam allowances, turn right side out, and press.

3. Baste the top edge of the flap to the top edge of the purse, with the wrong side of the flap facing the zipper. Open the zipper a short distance. (Fig. 3)

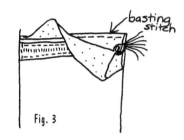

Fig. 3

4. Fold up the other end of the purse fabric, with the right sides meeting, and pin the three sides of the purse together. (Fig. 4)

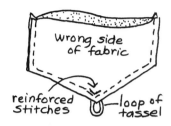

Fig. 4

5. Sew the three sides, using a 1/4" seam allowance, and being careful to avoid catching the edges of the flap in the seamlines. As described in the Techniques section on page 7, fold the bottom corners to form a triangle. Sew 2" across each triangle. (Fig. 5)

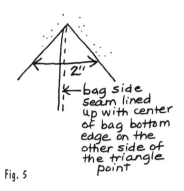

Fig. 5

Turn the purse right side out through the zipper opening and press. Add a cord or ribbon to the zipper head for ease in opening and closing.

Tapestry Bag

1. Refer to the Anything Bag instructions on page 8. Cut the fabric 11" x 18". Sew the zipper 1-1/2" below the top 11" edge. Cut a piece of fabric 3" x 12" for the bag handle. Use the easy handle method described on page 17 to fold, press, and sew a purse handle above the zipper and 3" from each edge of the bag. (Fig. 6)

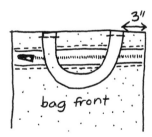

Fig. 6

2. Meet the two 11" edges of the fabric together with the right sides facing. Pin the three sides together and sew, as described in Step 5 for the Elegant Black Purse.

3. For the wider bottom surface of this bag, sew a 4" line across the triangle formed at each bottom corner of the bag, as described in the Techniques section on page 7. Also sew a 1" line across each top corner triangle of the bag. (Fig. 7)

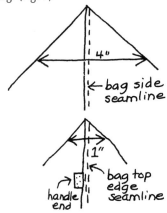

FELT PURSE

1. Refer to the Anything Bag instructions on pages 8-9. On the tissue pattern sheets, locate the pieces for the Special Occasion Flared Edge Purse and Top Flap. Cut two of each pattern piece from felt. To make the felt stronger, fuse interfacing to the wrong side of the purse front or back. I used tricot knit interfacing.

2. Sew a zipper 1" below the top edge of one purse front, using the Exposed Zipper method on page 8, and cutting away the felt behind the zipper.

3. With the wrong sides of the felt together, sew around the two layers of

the flap with a 1/4" seam allowance, leaving the straight edge open. Trim the seam allowances with pinking shears. Sew the straight edge to the top of the purse front with the zipper attached. (Fig. 8)

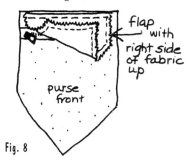

Fig. 8

4. Weave a purse handle from satin cord, or cut a handle from felt. Sew the ends at the edge of the top flap and on the purse front. (Fig. 9)

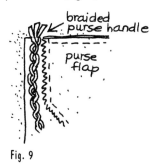

Fig. 9

5. Open the zipper a short distance. Place the purse back fabric with the right side facing the purse front. Sew around all the sides, being careful to avoid stitching on the purse handle or flap. Sew across the triangle formed at the bottom point of the purse to give depth to the bag. (Fig. 10)

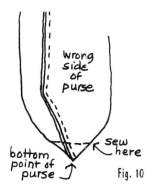

Fig. 10

6. Turn the purse right side out through the zipper opening. Use the flap area to showcase your special pins. You may also wish to hand sew a snap closure on the wrong side of the flap and on the purse.

Each of these bags has easy-to-sew features. They are perfect little purses for the high school prom. Consider hosting a pre-prom party for high school girls to sew their own handbags. Other projects to make for use at the prom are the fringed shawl (page 52) and gloves (page 72).

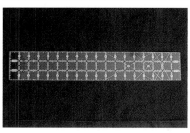

The 3″ x 18″ Omnigrid see-through ruler is a handy tool for cutting many of the 3″ purse and bag handles in this book.

Shopping Tote & Purse

This bag has a pleasing shape and it's easy to carry. Two sizes are provided on the tissue pattern sheets. See another example of the small version on the front cover of the book. The larger of the two bags is made from a rug. Make sure to use an appropriate sewing machine needle. I used a size 100 needle to accommodate the thickness of the rug.

Choose a sturdy fabric for this shapely tote or purse. On the left, the tote size bag is made from a rug and features a loop and button closure on the top. The smaller version on the right is sized as a purse and includes a zipper closure inside the top of the bag. Button by JHB International. Pink purse and lining fabrics by Dan River.

Supply List:

3/4 yd. sturdy fabric, 45" wide
  or fabric with crisp interfacing applied
  or a 20" x 28" rug
1/2 yd. fabric for bag lining and lining pockets
60" webbing for larger tote handles, 32" for smaller tote
Ultrasuede scraps for handle end covers

large button and 8" of cord or strip of Ultrasuede for
  bag closure
fusible spray such as Sulky KK2000
Optional:
  zipper for bag top closure - 18" for larger tote, 16"
    for smaller tote

1. On the tissue pattern sheets, locate the pieces for the Shopping Purse or Shopping Tote, bottom, and handle end cover. Cut two bag shapes and the corresponding bottom oval from fabric. Interface, if necessary. If using a rug or fabric that frays quickly, serge or zigzag around all pieces immediately to prevent uncontrollable raveling. Ask me why I recommend this...

2. Decorate or monogram the bag front and/or back. Sew the bag front and back together with right sides facing and 1/4" seam allowances. Mark quarter portions on the bag bottom opening and the oval bottom piece. Pin together with right sides facing and sew. The oval bottom gives this bag its shape. (Fig. 1)

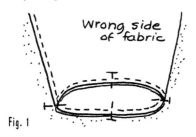

Fig. 1

3. Sew the handle ends to the bag, placing the ends 5" from the sides and 3" down from the top. (Fig. 2)

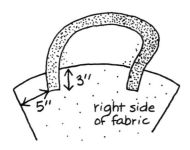

Fig. 2

For the smaller bag, place the handle ends 5" in and 2" down. Cut four Ultrasuede pieces for the handle end covers. Use fusible spray on the back of the pieces and place the pieces over the handle ends and sew around them. Pin the loops of the handles to the bag front and back to keep them out of the way while you sew the lining to the bag.

4. Cut two lining pieces using the bag shape as a guide but extending the sides as shown. (Fig. 3)

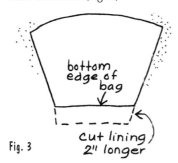

Fig. 3

If you want pockets in the bag lining, cut them out and sew them on. Sew the two lining pieces together along the sides only, with the right sides of the fabric facing and 1/4" seam allowances. Press. Slide the lining over the top of the bag with the right side of the lining facing the right side of the bag. Offset the lining and bag side seams slightly, pin the lining into place around the top of the bag, and sew with 1/4" seam allowances.

5. Turn the lining right side out, press the seamline, then insert the lining inside the bag. Sew 1/2" around the top of the bag to secure the lining to the bag. (Fig. 4)

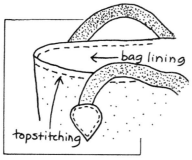

Fig. 4

Pull the lining out of the bag, turn under the open, raw edges and stitch them together. Insert the lining back inside the bag. Although the lining is slightly larger than the bag shape, it will settle inside the bag.

6. Sew a cord loop or a strip of Ultrasuede in a loop over the bag opening and add a large button as a closure, as shown on the larger bag.

7. Another way to close this bag is to sew a zipper insert. Measure the top open edge of the bag and select a zipper slightly shorter. Nylon zippers can be shortened to any length by stitching across the zipper at the desired length.

8. Cut two 2-1/2"-wide strips of bag lining fabric 2" longer than the zipper. Fold and press the strips in half lengthwise, right side out. Sew each strip to the right side of the zipper with the raw edges of the strip meeting the zipper edge and with 1" of fabric extending beyond the zipper ends. (Fig. 5)

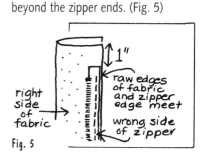

Fig. 5

Try the zipper unit in the bag opening to check the fit. Then sew the two strips together at each end to form the continuous fabric edge to sew to the top of the bag. (Fig. 6)

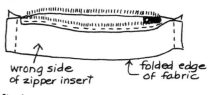

Fig. 6

Pin the folded edges of the zipper unit to the top edge of the bag. Sew from the right side of the bag to maintain a neat seamline on the outside of the bag. Now your shopping bag has a secured top closure.

Options:
* Add an extra layer of fabric to the bottom of the bag for extra strength. For the bag made from a rug, I used an interfaced piece of Ultrasuede for a durable and strong bottom surface.

Window Screen Crossover Bag

Try an unusual source of fabric for this bag: fiberglass window screen from the hardware store. You'll find it to be strong, supple, and easy to sew. If you prefer another fabric, the bag is a good choice for canvas, tapestry, or other durable fabrics.

Pack for a trip to the pool with this window screen bag - a quick glance lets you see the contents to make sure you haven't forgotten anything. All the edges of the bag are trimmed with different colors of bias tape. The shoulder strap makes it easy to carry the bag and a wet swimsuit and towel inside won't harm the bag fabric!

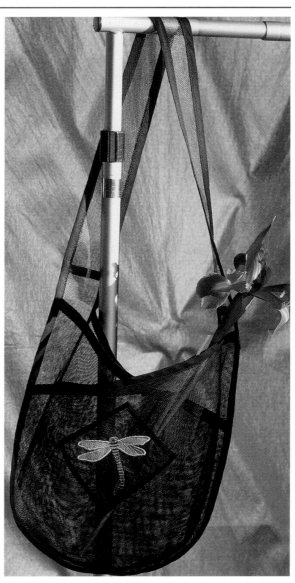

Window screen makes a semi-sheer fabric for this tote bag. Black bias tape covers all the edges and an appliqued/embroidered design I created for Cactus Punch trims the bag front. This versatile bag is also fun to use just because it's made from window screen.

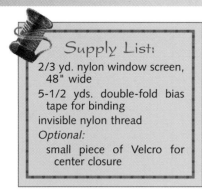

1. On the tissue pattern sheets, locate the piece for the Window Screen Crossover Bag and cut four from the nylon screen. Notice that two sizes of bags are shown on the pattern.

2. Cut a 3" x 36" strip for the sides of the bag and a 3" x 30" strip for the bag handle.

3. Sew bias binding to the diagonal edges of the four bag sections. One of my bags features all different colors of binding (a good way to use leftovers) and the other has black binding on all the bag edges. Clear nylon thread is a good choice for a bag with a variety of binding colors. Stitch with a narrow zigzag stitch or a straight stitch.

4. Line up two alternating bag sections, right sides up, and pin the edges together. Sew 1/4" from the edges to anchor the two layers together. Do this once for the front and once for the back side of the bag. (Fig. 1)

Fig. 1

5. With the right sides of the bag front and side section facing out, pin and sew the side section to the bag front. Use a 1/4" seam allowance or sew a narrower seam if you are using narrow (standard width) bias tape. (Fig. 2)

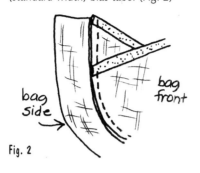

bag side

bag front

Fig. 2

Pin and sew the bag back to the other edge of the side section.

6. For a bag handle that rests smoothly on the shoulder, taper the width of the handle to 2" at the center. (Fig. 3)

← 2" →

← 3" →

Fig. 3

Now sew the handle ends to the edges of the side sections or the bag. (Fig. 4)

bag handle

bag side

Fig. 4

7. Wrap the seam allowance with bias binding, sew the binding in place, then sew the loose edge of the bias to the handle strip. This will insure a firm attachment of the handle to the bag. (Fig. 5)

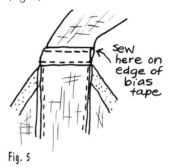

sew here on edge of bias tape

Fig. 5

8. Sew bias binding around each side of the bag and handle. This will be two continuous seams. Start and overlap the bias binding in a straight section of the bag edge. Use a narrow zigzag stitch.

Options:

* Decorate your window screen bag with embroidery also done on screen or add an applique.

* Sew on small pieces of Velcro at the center point of the bag where the diagonal edges intersect and the front and back meet.

When you buy screen at the hardware store and mention that you'll be sewing it into a bag, watch the expression on the face of the store employee. This non-standard use for screen will convince people that you are quite clever... or crazy!

Ultrasuede Belt Purse

Keep your purse on your body at all times by sliding it onto a belt. This trim and simple Ultrasuede bag holds the bare necessities while worn on your body. Add an applique, monogram, or embroidery for a classy touch.

Keep hands and shoulders free by wearing this small purse on your belt. I chose Ultrasuede as a strong and stylish fabric for this project. Notice the colorful tassel that serves as a zipper pull and the extra fabric tabs at each end of the zipper. These small details make it easier to open and close the zipper. Look closely and you'll see another of Sarah's quilts in the background. I'm lucky to have a sister who makes wonderful quilts. Tassel by Wrights.

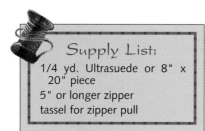
1. On the tissue pattern sheets, locate the two pieces for the Ultrasuede Belt Purse. Cut one front and one back from Ultrasuede. Also cut a casing 1-3/4" wide and 4-1/2" long.

2. On the back of the purse front, draw lines 1-1/4" from the top edge and 1" from each side. Place and pin the zipper, right side down, along the line parallel with the top edge. Sew around the two long sides and bottom end of the zipper, starting and stopping 1" from each side of the purse. (Fig. 1)

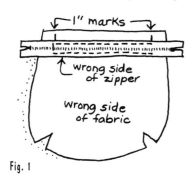

Fig. 1

Remove from the sewing machine and pull the zipper head down within the stitching lines. Then sew across the open end of the zipper, using the 1" line marker as a guide.

3. Carefully cut the fabric from the front of the zipper area. Sew 5/8" square tabs at each end of the zipper on the right side of the bag to make it easy to grab, open, and close the zipper. (Fig. 2) If the seams across the ends of the zipper aren't your neatest work, the tabs will cover it up.

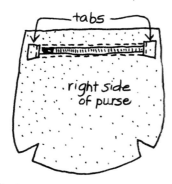

Fig. 2

4. Sew the two darts on the bottom of the purse front. Make sure the stitching closes the darts.

5. Sew on the casing to slide the belt through on the back of the purse. (You may want to adjust the casing width for narrower or wider belts.) Pin or tape the casing on the purse back 1" below the top edge. Sew the casing to the

purse with 1/8" seam allowances. Make the stitching strong by sewing the seams twice. (Fig. 3)

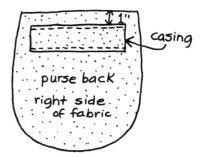

Fig. 3

6. Open the zipper part way and pin the purse front and back pieces with right sides together. Sew around the edges with a 1/2" seam allowance. Use a Teflon coated presser foot or a roller foot on the sewing machine for best results with Ultrasuede. Clip and trim the seams and turn the purse right side out through the zipper opening.

7. To flatten the seams, press the purse with a press cloth over it to prevent impressing the Ultrasuede with the bottom of the iron.

8. Tie a tassel or a piece of ribbon to the zipper head.

Slide this small purse onto your belt, add your supplies, and enjoy the freedom of a purse that stays with you and doesn't fall off your shoulder!

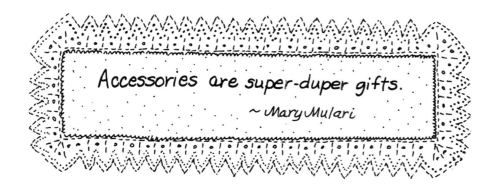

Accessories are super-duper gifts.

~ Mary Mulari

Japanese Fan Bag

This shapely bag was designed by Terri Johnson. She combined some of her favorite Japanese fabric prints with decorative stitching, machine embroidery, and the quilting fan shape to create a unique purse for a special occasion.

On the back of the fan bag, add a special machine embroidery design for additional interest and trim. Terri stitched this embroidery design on a Husqvarna Viking embroidery sewing machine.

Combine quilting and kimono fabrics to make this clever and shapely bag. A variety of decorative machine stitches adds interest between the sections of the fan design.

Supply List:

- 1/3 yd. navy cotton fabric, 45" wide
- 4 pieces Japanese print fabrics, 4" x 8" each
- 10" x 18" fabric for bag lining - either print or solid
- 1/4 yd. red fabric, 45" wide
- 10" x 18" piece thin cotton batting
- 1/3 yd. fusible knit interfacing
- red and navy thread (Terri recommends 50 wt. cotton)
- water-soluble stabilizer for machine embroidery

1. On the tissue pattern sheets, locate the pieces for the Japanese Fan Bag Scallop Edge, Half Circle, and Wedge. Using the wedge shape, cut four print and three solid navy fan wedges. With 1/4" seam allowances, sew the wedges together, starting with a print and alternating prints and solids. (Fig. 1) Press each seam as you go.

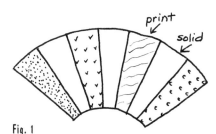

Fig. 1

2. Fuse the knit interfacing to the batting, then flip the batting over so you're working on the other side and the interfacing is on the bottom. Pin or use fusible spray to secure the fan to the batting, aligning one edge of the fan with the center of the batting. (Fig. 2)

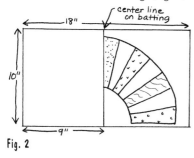

Fig. 2

Sew on each seamline of the fan wedges, using decorative stitches. Press after stitching.

3. Cut a 10" square of navy fabric for the bag back. Place the right side of the fabric over the fan and align one edge of the fabric with the center line. Sew the square to the fan along the center line. Press the seam and flip the square to cover the batting on the left. (Fig. 3)

Fig. 3

4. Pin the half circle pattern on the red fabric. Cut 1/4" larger all around the pattern. Turn under 1/4" and press the curved side. (Fig. 4)

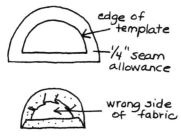

Fig. 4

Pin the half circle, right side up, over the raw edges of the bottom of the fan block and extending to the navy square. Sew the curved edge in place with a blanket stitch, using navy thread. (Fig. 5)

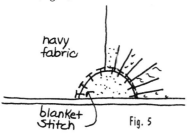

Fig. 5

5. With the scallop edge pattern, trace the scallops and straight edges onto both sides of the bag, pieced and solid. It's easiest to trace on the interfaced side of the batting and use the stitching lines to guide the pattern placement. (Fig. 6)

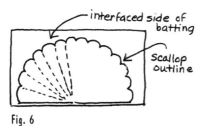

Fig. 6

6. Pin the lining fabric to the right side of the bag with the right sides of the fabric facing. Flip the piece over and sew along the bottom and scalloped edges traced on the interfacing. Leave a 3" to 4" opening on the straight bottom edge for turning. (Fig. 7)

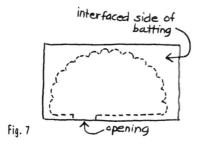

Fig. 7

Trim and clip the seam allowances. Press, turn right side out, and press the seams again.

7. Straight stitch down the center line of the block along the seamline and through all the layers. (Fig. 8) Hand sew the opening closed.

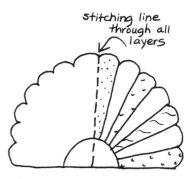

Fig. 8

8. To add machine embroidery to the navy back of the bag, hoop two layers of water-soluble stabilizer, spray the stabilizer with fusible spray, and center the navy side of the bag on the stabilizer. Stitch the design and remove the fabric from the hoop. Remove as much stabilizer as possible.

9. Fold the bag in half with the right sides out and matching up the scallops. Using smoke tone invisible thread, zigzag the open sides together.

10. For the bag handles, cut a strip of red fabric 1" x 27". Fold in half lengthwise and sew right sides together with a 1/4" seam allowance. Turn the strip right side out. (Terri recommends a Mini Fasturn tool for this step.) Cut the strip in two 13-1/2" pieces. Press. Pin and sew the handles to the scalloped edges of the bag. For a bag closure, sew a snap or Velcro inside the top edge of the bag.

Isn't this a great way to combine special fabrics with quilting and machine embroidery? Have fun with this bag!

Day-Trip Shoulder Bag

I saw a bag like this one in an airport on one of my seminar trips. It makes good sense as a lightweight bag for a day long shopping trip or day of touring. Instead of using leather, I chose a tapestry print fabric for its sturdy quality and the colorful surface to camouflage marks and stains. Both the bag front and back have pockets for extra storage and the handle can be made just the right length for you. Besides all of that, it's a quick and easy bag to sew.

Fold down the top opening of this bag and close it with an elastic loop (a ponytail elastic wrap is used on this bag). Make the shoulder strap the length you find most comfortable. Piping sewn between the front and back of the bag adds a subtle touch of class. Hidden features of this bag include a zipper pocket under the top flap and an open pocket on the back of the bag. Piping and tassels by Wrights. Button by JHB International.

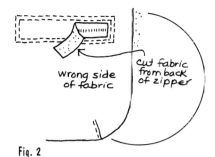

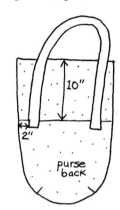

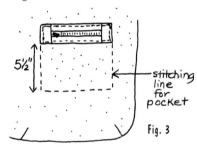

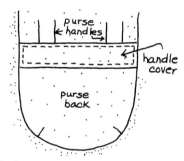

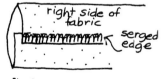

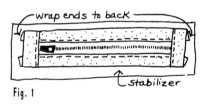

Supply List:

- 1 yd. of tapestry or other substantial fabric, 45" wide or wider
- or lighter weight fabric with crisp interfacing to give added support
- 7" zipper
- 1/2 yd. decorative braid to frame the zipper
- 50" piping
- 9" x 3" piece tear-away stabilizer
- 9" x 7" fabric piece for pocket lining
- invisible nylon thread

1. On the tissue pattern sheets, locate the piece for the Day-Trip Shoulder Bag and cut two from fabric. Sew the darts at the rounded corners on the bag back and front. Reinforce the stitching. If the fabric you've chosen ravels easily, you may want to serge or zigzag stitch around all the edges at this time.

2. To prepare the zipper frame to sew to the bag front, sew strips of decorative braid to the two long sides of the zipper, sewing over a piece of tear-away stabilizer. Sew a piece of the braid, with raw edges turned under, over the short ends of the zipper to complete the frame. (Fig. 1)

Fig. 1

Remove the stabilizer and pin the frame to the right side of the bag front 9" from the top straight edge. Sew around the outer edges with a zigzag or straight stitch, then sew a second row of stitching over the inside edges of the trim. Cut away the fabric covering the zipper teeth from the wrong side of the fabric. (Fig. 2)

Fig. 2

3. Zigzag or serge the edges of the pocket lining fabric. Pin the fabric, with the right side facing the wrong side of the bag front, behind the zipper opening. The top edge should align with the top edge of the zipper frame. On the bag front, draw vertical lines extending 5-1/2" down on each side of the frame and a horizontal line connecting them. (Fig. 3)

Fig. 3

Sew on these lines and across the top of the zipper frame to attach the pocket backing. If you use clear nylon thread, on most fabrics this seam will be invisible.

4. Cut a piece of fabric 3" x 36" for the bag handle. Zigzag or serge along one long edge. Fold in 1" along the unstitched long edge, wrong sides facing, and overlap the raw edge with the serged edge and press. (Fig. 4)

Fig. 4

Sew through the serged stitching to hold the layers together. This is a fast

way to make a handle that doesn't involve turning the fabric right side out.

5. On the bag back, draw a horizontal line 10" from the top edge of the fabric. Place and pin the ends of the bag handle just beyond the line and 2" from the bag sides. (Fig. 5)

Fig. 5

Put the bag on your shoulder to test the handle length. Make adjustments to the length and then sew the handle ends to the bag.

Cut a piece of fabric 10" wide and 2-1/2" high for the handle ends cover. Turn under and press both 10" edges. Pin the fabric on the line drawn on the bag back and over the handle ends. Sew the cover fabric in place. (Fig. 6)

Fig. 6

6. I added a pocket to the back of the bag below the handle cover piece. Cut a piece of fabric 8-1/2" wide and 7" high (or size this pocket to suit your own needs). Serge or zigzag one of the 8-1/2" edges. Turn under and press the pocket sides and bottom. Turn under 1" at the top serged edge, press, and sew. Position and pin the pocket beneath the bottom edge of the handle cover on the bag back. Sew to attach, reinforcing the stitches at the top edges of the pocket. (Fig. 7)

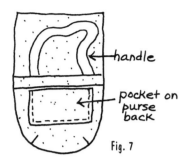

handle

pocket on purse back

Fig. 7

7. Piping adds a touch of style around the outer edges of this bag and I recommend you add it to your bag too. Of course it's not a requirement, but it is a subtle trim that's easy to add. Make your own piping, or purchase a package. Sew the piping around the right side of the front of the bag, making

sure that the bobbin thread color can be seen easily on the wrong side of the fabric. (Fig. 8) If your sewing machine has a special presser foot recommended for sewing on piping, this is the time to use it.

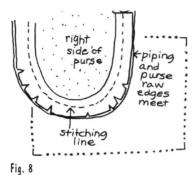

right side of purse

piping and purse raw edges meet

stitching line

Fig. 8

8. Pin the bag back to the front with right sides facing. Use the stitching line from attaching the piping to the bag front as a guide for sewing the front and back together.

9. Turn the bag right side out and press the edges to flatten. Turn the top open

edges under 1", press, and sew. Sew a button to the bag front and sew a loop with cord or use a ponytail elastic circle, as I did, for the loop which is sewn to the bag top edge. (Fig. 9) I added tassels to the button for extra trim.

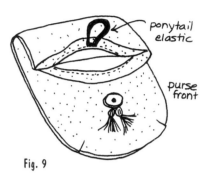

ponytail elastic

purse front

Fig. 9

Here's hoping you'll enjoy using this lightweight, practical, and stylish bag inspired by the one I saw in the airport. You never know where a sewing inspiration will appear!

Here's the bulletin board in my sewing room. The sketch and notes for the Day-Trip Shoulder Bag were pinned here until I began to work on this book. What you see now is a mixture of ideas and memorabilia.

Jeans Pockets Purse

Remember when they used to call purses pocketbooks? Maybe that dates me! This pocketbook was designed by Luveta Nickels whose specialty is making clever things from old jeans. Luveta said, "I thought about the essentials for a girl's purse and how to accommodate them in a handy way. On the front, my lipstick, sunglasses, and cell phone are labeled and easy to find." The handle is braided flat-felled seams from two pairs of jeans.

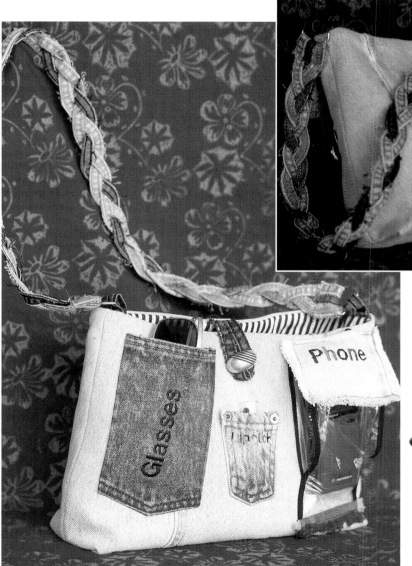

The back of the Jeans Pockets Purse has an embroidered jeans watch pocket ready to hold the car keys. Of course, you can make and label pockets for any supplies of your choice.

Here's a clever purse made by cutting up and sewing together parts of old jeans. The three front pockets store a girl's essential supplies and they are labeled with machine embroidered lettering.

Supply List:
2 pairs of jeans - 1 blue, 1 black
3/4 yd. lining fabric
2 yds. fusible interfacing
1/4 yd. clear vinyl
2 "D" rings, 1-1/4"
large button
1 yd. double-fold bias tape
1/4 yd. tear-away stabilizer
90/14 denim needle
assorted rayon thread for machine embroidery

1. Wash and iron the two pairs of jeans you'll use for this project.

2. From the black pair of jeans, tear off one back pocket for the glasses pocket and also remove the watch pocket for the keys pocket. Cut one piece 1-1/2" wide and 4-1/2" long for the fringed trim at the bottom of the phone pocket. Remove four belt loops and cut away the flat-felled (double stitched) seam from one side of the jeans leg.

3. From the blue jeans, remove the watch pocket for the lipstick pocket, cut a pocket flap 5" x 6-1/2". On the tissue pattern sheets, locate the piece for the Jeans Pocket Purse and cut one as shown. (Fig. 1) Also cut two flat-felled leg seams the full length of the leg.

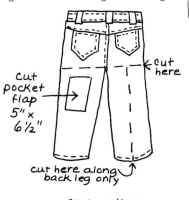

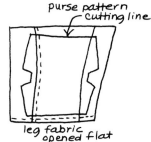

Fig. 1

4. Fringe about 1/2" on all four sides of the pocket flap. Fuse a piece of interfacing to the wrong side of the flap in the solid, non-fringed area. (Fig. 2)

Fig. 2

Also fuse interfacing to the wrong side of the entire bag fabric piece.

5. Now it's time to add machine embroidered labels to the pockets and pocket flap. Luveta recommends basting pockets to a larger piece of fabric and then positioning the fabric in the machine's embroidery hoop. Practice to get the word placement right before stitching on the pockets. Stitch the words GLASSES, PHONE, LIPSTICK, and KEYS on the appropriate pockets. Refer to the photo of the purse for lettering and pocket choices.

6. Cut a piece of clear vinyl 10" x 7-1/2". Fold under 1/2" on one 10" edge and fold under again. Topstitch in place, using a Teflon or walking foot for stitching ease, and finger press. (No irons here!) Wrap and sew the outer 7-1/2" edges with double-fold bias tape, then fold the vinyl as illustrated to a 4" front width and sew bias tape to the foldlines. (Fig. 3)

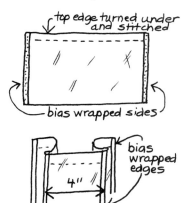

Fig. 3

Topstitch the outside bias edges to the denim purse using the placement lines on the pattern, and then make a pleat in the vinyl sides to line up the inside set of bias edges with the ones sewn to the fabric. Sew up 2" from the bottom of the vinyl through all the layers of bias and purse fabric. (Fig. 4)

Fig. 4

The top will be open to form a gusset to accommodate the phone. Fringe the black denim strip 1/2" on all sides and fold it in half along the short edges to sew over the bottom edge of the vinyl. Fold the top flap you cut from the blue jeans in half with the wrong sides together and the 5" edges meeting. Stitch just inside the fringe on all three sides. (Fig. 5)

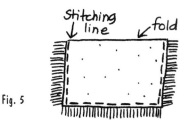

Fig. 5

Topstitch the flap to the purse front above the vinyl pocket and leave an opening for the phone antenna.

7. Sew the other three pockets to the purse in the locations shown on the pattern. The keys pocket will be on the back of the purse. If you cannot sew close enough to the rivets found on most jeans watch pockets, use the Jean-a-ma-jig to level the foot and tack at the side and top edges of the watch pockets to hold them in place. (Fig. 6)

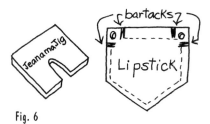

Fig. 6

8. With the right sides of the fabric together, stitch the sides of the purse together. Bring the center of the purse bottom to meet the side seam and stitch across the bottom. (Fig. 7) Do this on both sides of the purse.

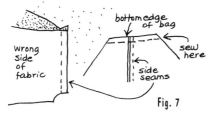

Fig. 7

9. Wrap two belt loops around each "D" ring and place them along each side of the purse's side seams and stitch in place. Center a 7" looped strip of black flat-felled seam on the back top edge of the purse and sew it in place. (Fig. 8)

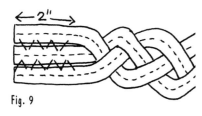

Fig. 8

10. To make the purse handle, use two blue and one black flat-felled seams. Secure the first 2" on one end by zigzag stitching them together, as shown. (Fig. 9)

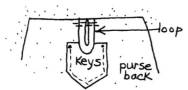

Fig. 9

Braid the three strands loosely and flat all the way to the ends of the seams. Test the handle length and shorten the handle if necessary. Zigzag the ends together at the other end.

(Luveta found that with use, this strap tends to stretch in length, so you may want to make the handle shorter than you want it to be.)

11. Fold the strap ends around the "D" rings and sew them to themselves with a triple zigzag stitch. Start sewing in the middle of the thick strap and stitch to the edges. Make sure the stitching is reinforced so the strap will carry the weight of all your STUFF! Turn the purse inside out and put the strap inside the purse. (Fig. 10)

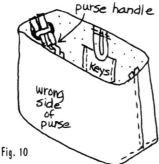

Fig. 10

12. Cut the purse lining using the purse pattern and also add a layer of fusible interfacing. Sew to the lining any inside pockets you've planned for the purse. Meeting the right sides of the fabric, sew down the sides of the lining using a slightly larger seam allowance than you did for the purse. Leave a 6" opening in one side. (Fig. 11) By using a slightly larger seam allowance, the lining will fit down into your purse more easily.

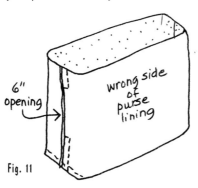

Fig. 11

13. Turn the lining right side out and insert it into the denim purse, with the right side of the lining facing the right side of the purse. Match the side seams of the lining and purse and stitch around the top edge. Be sure to keep the shoulder strap out of the stitching area. It will be inside your purse at this point.

14. Turn the entire purse through the side opening in the lining. Be patient as this is a bit of a job. Press the top edge of the purse and topstitch if desired. Watch out for that vinyl pocket! Machine or hand stitch the lining opening closed.

15. Sew a large button to the front and set the loop for the button by zigzag stitching above and below the opening needed for the button. (Fig. 12)

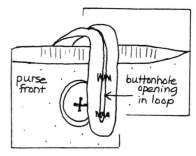

Fig. 12

Options:
* Straps or handles for this purse could be made from old leather belts or bands of denim cut from the jeans.

There are so many possibilities here... use your imagination and check out the jeans in your stash.

Scarves & Belts

M Scarf

Here's a scarf that's easy to wear and always looks well arranged. The shape is very unusual and I wasn't sure how to describe it until I held up the two square corners and the shape resembled an "M." (Fig. 1) I've adapted this pattern from my friend Rita Farro's version. She says it's one of the most popular pieces she shows in her gift seminar.

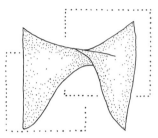

Fig. 1

Dorothy, Helen, and Elsie wear the M Scarf in three different ways. In any position, it knots and lies as an attractive frame for the face.

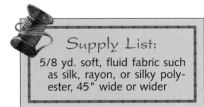

1. On the tissue pattern sheets, locate the piece for the M Scarf and position the scarf pattern on the folded fabric, as illustrated. (Fig. 2a) If you'd like to make the scarf from two different fabrics, layer the fabrics with both right sides up, as illustrated, in order to get two scarf shapes that can be sewn together in the correct position. (Fig. 2b) Soft, fluid fabrics should be placed on a firm flat surface for cutting. Don't let any of the fabric hang over a table edge. Pin the pattern to the fabric with many pins to prevent the fabric from shifting and to cut the pattern accurately. Cut two sets of the pattern from the fabric.

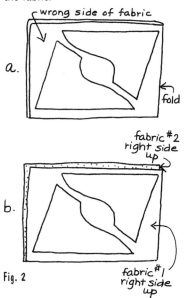

Fig. 2

2. Pin two sets of scarf halves together, right sides facing, along the short diagonal line. (Fig. 3)

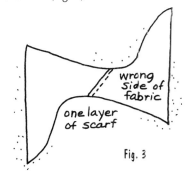

Fig. 3

Sew with a 1/4" seam allowance and trim and press the seams.

3. Match the right sides of both scarf halves together and pin first at the seamlines. Then pin the corners and points together and add additional pins between. (Fig. 4)

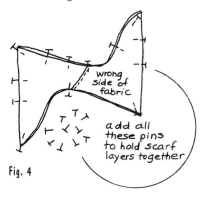

Fig. 4

4. Sew around the scarf with a 1/4" seam allowance, leaving a 2" opening on a straight edge to pull the scarf through. (Fig. 5)

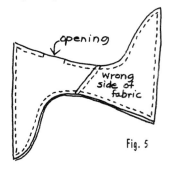

Fig. 5

Trim and clip the seam allowances with pinking shears. Press the seam and then turn the scarf right side out through the opening. Press around the scarf to flatten the seamline.

5. To wear this scarf, hold it by the end points and watch it twist on itself. Place it around your neck, tie the ends, and position the scarf to drape to the front, side, or back. The knot can lie on the shoulder or hang in the front. (Fig. 6)

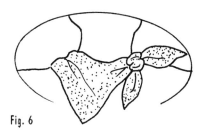

Fig. 6

Another way to wear it is to tie a loose knot in the middle of the scarf, fluff out the corners, and tie the ends behind your neck. (Fig. 7)

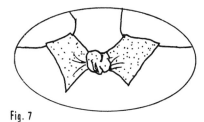

Fig. 7

For another view of this scarf, see my picture on page 5.

Trimming the seam allowances on this scarf is one of the many times you'll use pinking shears as you work on the projects in this book. Pinking Shears by Fiskars.

Buttonhole Scarf

My theory is that many women don't wear scarves because they don't feel confident tying them. This scarf is easy to put on and arrange. Make it in Polarfleece, in silky fabrics, even using two different fabrics so the scarf is reversible, or in taffeta-lined velveteen.

This is just the beginning of possibilities for the Buttonhole Scarf! On the far left and right, Elsie and Naomi are wearing Polarfleece versions of the scarf, great for keeping warm on a cold day. The scarf is also a great accessory for day or evening wear, as seen on Nancy, Lorraine, and Joan. Behind my model friends is Sarah's kaleidoscope quilt. Polarfleece from Malden Mills.

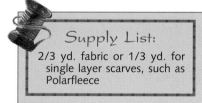

Supply List:
2/3 yd. fabric or 1/3 yd. for single layer scarves, such as Polarfleece

1. On the tissue paper pattern sheets, locate the piece for the Buttonhole Scarf. Note that the straight edge is placed along the fold of the fabric.
2. For silky, slippery fabrics, work on a large flat surface and place the right sides of the fabric together. Pin the pattern in place using many pins. Cut out the scarf layers and before moving the fabric, slide the pins under the pattern to pin just the fabric layers together. Use plenty of pins. Finally, unpin the pattern.
3. Use a new size 70 needle to sew around all the edges of the scarf using a 1/4" seam allowance. Sew from the

edge of the fabric to the seam allowance for a neat finish. Leave a 2" opening, sewing back to the outer edge of the fabrics, as illustrated. (Fig. 1)

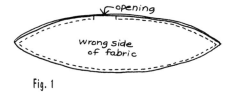

Fig. 1

Trim the seam allowances with pinking shears and press.

4. Turn the scarf right side out. Press the seamline all around the scarf. Hand sew or fuse the opening closed.

5. Sew two buttonholes on only one end of the scarf. The location is printed on the pattern, but you can adjust it. On thin fabrics, sew 1"-long buttonholes about 1" apart. Use tear-away stabilizer beneath the buttonhole area and remove it after stitching.

6. In Polarfleece, this scarf can become a no-sew accessory. For a more interesting edge, cut the scarf with a pinking shears or a wavy edge rotary cutter. The buttonholes can simply be cut - carefully - into the scarf.

7. Edge stitching adds an interesting dimension on Polarfleece. Use the same thread on top and in the bobbin of the machine. Experiment on scraps to find the right stitch for this project. One stitch that forms a scalloped edge on Polarfleece is a utility stitch shown. (Fig. 2)

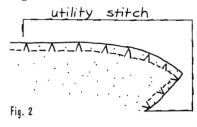

Fig. 2

Increase the top tension on the machine so the thread draws the edge of the fabric to form the scalloped edge. Also try an heirloom blanket stitch. (Fig. 3)

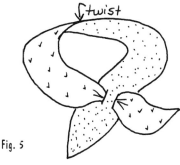

By experimenting with your machine and the fabric, you'll achieve the look you want. Then sew around the edges.

8. Space the buttonholes 1-1/2" apart. Sew traditional satin stitched buttonholes or sew a buttonhole outline if your machine has the option. Use stabilizer under the buttonholes and tear it away after stitching. (Fig. 4)

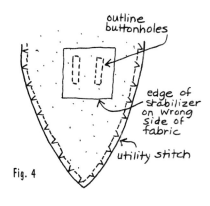

Fig. 4

Options:
* Use bias binding around the scarf edges, for a different edge finish.

After these easy steps, your scarf is done. To wear this scarf, place it around your neck and lace one end through the two buttonholes on the opposite end. For an interesting look, make the scarf of two different fabrics. When you wear it, twist it in the center back so the other side of the fabric will lace through the buttonholes on the front of the scarf. (Fig. 5)

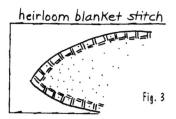

Fig. 5

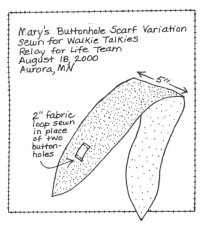

Walkie Talkie Team, American Cancer Society's Relay for Life, Aurora, Minnesota, August 18-19, 2000. Here's our team in the Relay t-shirts and the scarves I made, adapting the Buttonhole Scarf as you can see in the variation illustration above. We were proud to receive the team award for the most funds raised for the first-ever Relay in our town.

Crossover Belt

This belt has a lot of great features: it's easy to sew, comfortable to wear, adjustable after a big meal, and stylish too.

Supply List:
1/4 yd. durable fabric, 45"
    wide or wider
12" Velcro
string for measuring waistline
Optional:
    1/4 yd. fusible interfacing

A simple belt made from colorful striped fabric adds a bright accent to a plain dress. Thanks to Velcro, this belt is easy to wear and to adjust for comfort.

1. To make this belt, you need to measure your waist. But we'll do this in an unconventional way so there's no need to know your actual waist measurement! Wrap a string around your waist and add 10" to that length. Use this as the total length needed to make your belt. If the "string + 10" length is longer than the fabric is wide, plan to make the belt in two pieces with a seam at the center back. I credit Rita Farro with introducing the idea of using the string method for waist measurement.

2. Decide on the width of your finished belt. The striped belt pictured is 2" wide so I cut the fabric 4-1/2" wide to make the belt, its self-lining, and 1/2" for seam allowance. Cloth belts that are narrow tend to get less distorted and creased in body folds when they are worn... just a little food for thought!

3. After cutting (and possibly piecing) the fabric for your belt, press the belt in half lengthwise with the right side of the fabric out. Try the belt around your waist to determine if the fabric needs the extra support of fusible interfacing which you will add at this time. On the side of the belt that will be the lining, sew a 6" length of the loop (soft) side of Velcro 5" from each end. (Fig. 1)

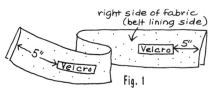

Fig. 1

4. Turn the belt wrong sides out and sew the length of the fabric together with a 1/4" seam allowance. (Fig. 2)

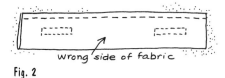

Fig. 2

Turn right side out and press.

At the belt ends, fold and pin a pleat about the width of the Velcro. (Fig. 3)

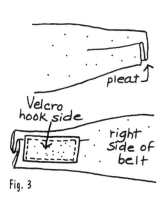

Fig. 3

Cut two 1-1/2" pieces of the hook side of Velcro. Sew each one over the pleated areas at the ends of the belt, sewing on the right (non-lining) side of the belt.

5. Try the belt on. Wrap each end of the belt to the wrong side to catch the Velcro surfaces together. See, I told you it would be easy to make - and comfortable too. (Fig. 4)

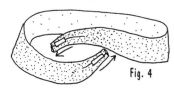

Fig. 4

Lock & Loop Belt

A band with Velcro on one end of the belt slides through the loop on the other end and locks with the matching Velcro sewn to the belt front. It's a clever closure that's easy to sew. Add a secret pocket on the inside of the belt to store and hide money or a key.

Shown on Sarah's wall hanging are two versions of the Lock & Loop Belt. As a special feature, a pocket sewn to the back lining of the blue belt holds and hides money. The pink belt is a single layer of belting and is also featured on the cover of the book.

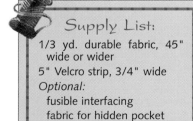

Supply List:
1/3 yd. durable fabric, 45" wide or wider
5" Velcro strip, 3/4" wide
Optional:
fusible interfacing
fabric for hidden pocket

1. Determine the belt length with the "string + 10" method: Wrap a string around your waist and add 10" to that length. (Fig. 1)

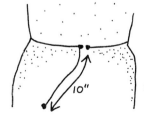

"string plus 10" method of waist measuring

10"

Fig. 1

If the fabric width is shorter than "string + 10," plan to cut two sections of belt fabric and seam them at the center back.

2. The blue belt pictured is 2-3/4" wide. The fabric cut for the belt was 6" wide. Decide on the finished width for your own belt and cut the fabric double the width plus 1/2" for seam allowances.

3. Press the fabric in half lengthwise with the wrong sides together. Try the belt around your waist to determine if you need to fuse interfacing to the fabric to give it more body. If it's needed, fuse interfacing to the entire width and length of the belt or to half of the width, fusing to the wrong side of the fabric.

4. If you want to add the hidden pocket to the belt lining, prepare and sew it at this time. I cut a piece of fabric 3" x 8", turned under and pressed the four edges, and sewed across the top edge, also attaching a narrow 2" strip of the hook (rough) side of Velcro to the pocket edge. (Fig. 2)

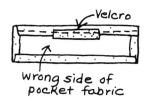

Fig. 2

Next, sew the three sides of the pocket to the belt lining. Sew the loop (soft) side of the Velcro to the belt to match up with the Velcro placement on the pocket. (Fig. 3)

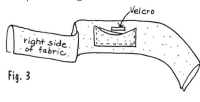

Fig. 3

5. Turn the belt fabric wrong side out, pin the long sides together, and mark one end to taper the belt. Draw lines from the 5" point on the belt sides to 1" center points at the end of the belt. (Fig. 4)

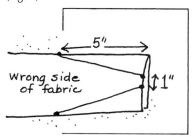

Fig. 4

Sew along all the edges of the belt with a 1/4" seam allowance, leaving an opening for turning the belt right side out and sewing along the lines drawn to create one narrower belt end. (Fig. 5)

Fig. 5

Trim the seam allowances with pinking shears, press the seam, and turn the belt right side out.

6. To form the loop on the square end of the belt, mark a foldline 4-1/2" from the end. Turn and twist the end of the fabric to form a loop. (Fig. 6)

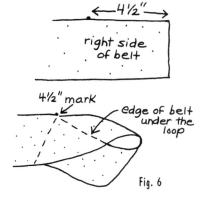

Fig. 6

Note that this end of the belt will be pinned and sewn to the belt front at an angle. (Fig. 7)

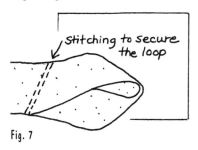

Fig. 7

7. It's best to try the belt on now to plan the most comfortable location for the Velcro on the tapered end. Cut a 3" piece of the loop (soft) side of Velcro and a 1-1/2" piece of the hook (rough) side. See the illustration for the location of each piece on the belt, but make sure this works for your belt. (Fig. 8)

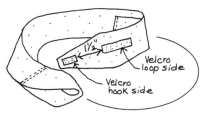

Fig. 8

Sew the two pieces onto the right side of the belt. Then put it on and lock the belt through the loop.

Options:
* Use the same loop & lock technique on a piece of belting, as shown on the pink belt.

Won't this be a great belt to wear to lunch when you order dessert too?

Wraps to Wear

Cowl Poncho for All Reasons

Make this poncho for use on rainy days or cold weather. When it's made from water-repellent nylon, it provides protection from the rain and stores folded in its own pocket. Made from Polarfleece, the poncho keeps you warm with its drawstring cowl neckline. Make both versions and you'll be prepared for all kinds of weather.

Enjoy wearing the cowl poncho in all kinds of weather. On the left, Helen's poncho features a front hand warmer pocket and the cowl worn as a collar. Naomi's cowl is shown on her head, working as a hood. Lorraine's Polarfleece poncho has a shorter cowl collar with a drawstring neckline. Polarfleece by Malden Mills.

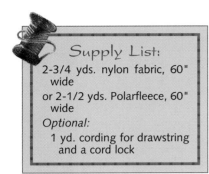

Supply List:

2-3/4 yds. nylon fabric, 60"
 wide

or 2-1/2 yds. Polarfleece, 60"
 wide

Optional:

 1 yd. cording for drawstring
 and a cord lock

1. On the tissue pattern sheets, locate the piece for the Cowl Poncho. Place and pin the pattern on the fabric with folds at the shoulder and center front and back, as indicated on the pattern. (Fig. 1)

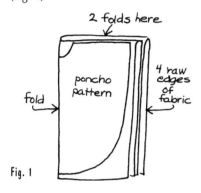

Fig. 1

Cut the neck opening and then unfold the fabric at the shoulder line so you can cut a deeper opening, as indicated on the pattern, for the front neck opening. Add the notch to indicate the center front of the poncho. (Fig. 2)

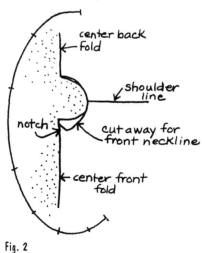

Fig. 2

2. For the tall cowl that extends to become a hood on the nylon poncho, cut a piece of nylon on the fold with the measurements indicated on the illustration. (Fig. 3)

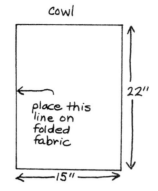

Fig. 3

You may want to try on the cowl by pinning or basting the 22" edges together and slipping it over your head. Adjust the length at this time if you want a shorter cowl. Then sew the 22" edges together with the right sides of the fabric facing and using a 1/4" seam allowance. Serge or zigzag the seam allowance to prevent fraying. For the Polarfleece shorter cowl, cut the cowl 12" tall instead of 22".

Turn under, press, and topstitch around one open end of the cowl. Turn it into a casing and insert a drawstring, as seen on the Polarfleece poncho. Cut two small eyelet holes 1-1/2" below the cowl top edge and centered with the seamline, which will be at the center front. Then turn under the Polarfleece 1" and hem. (Fig. 4)

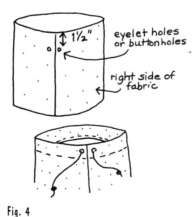

Fig. 4

Thread a cord or ribbon through the casing and add a cord lock or tie the two cords together in a knot.

3. Decide where to place the cowl seamline in the poncho neckline. If you want a more water-repellent cowl, place the seamline at the shoulder line or center front rather than the center back where rain would come through the seamline. Pin and sew the cowl to the poncho neckline, meeting the right sides of the fabric. Serge or zigzag the seam allowances and topstitch the seam allowances to the poncho body, as illustrated. (Fig. 5)

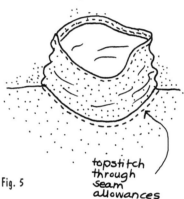

Fig. 5

4. Try the poncho on to test the fit over your arms and body. Trim the edges if you want less coverage over the ends of your arms and hands. Zigzag or serge the outer edge of the poncho. On the Polarfleece, serging helps to flatten the edge of the fabric for a neater finish. Turn the serged/zigzagged edge 1/4" to the wrong side of the fabric, pin, and sew in place. Press the nylon fabric edges. On Polarfleece, you won't need to press. Your poncho is ready to wear.

5. Add a front hand warmer pocket to the poncho front. On the tissue pattern sheets, locate the piece for the Cowl Poncho Hand Warmer Pocket and cut from folded fabric. Serge or zigzag the pocket edges. Turn under 1/4" on all four sides and press. Try the poncho on to decide the best location for the pocket. Sew to the poncho by sewing two seams across the top edge and leaving hand openings on each side of the pocket, as illustrated. (Fig. 6)

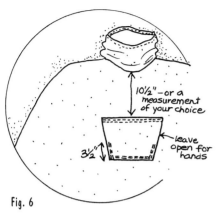

Fig. 6

This pocket is shown with the wide end up on the nylon poncho to prevent rain from coming in the pocket. It can also be sewn on with the narrower end up if you're not worried about rain!

6. Add a nylon self-storage pocket to the back of the nylon poncho. Cut a piece of nylon fabric 13" x 9". Serge or zigzag all four edges. Turn under and press the edges, sewing across the top

edge to secure it to the pocket. Pin the pocket to the center bottom edge of the back of the poncho with the pocket top edge lined up with the poncho bottom. (Fig. 7)

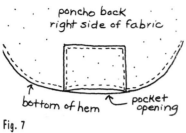

Fig. 7

Sew around the three pocket edges to attach it to the poncho, reinforcing the stitches at the top corners.

7. To fit the poncho in the pocket, place the poncho flat with the front side up. Fold in the poncho sides to line up with the pocket edges. Fold down the cowl. Fold the pocket to the top and fold the poncho in sections down to fit into the pocket. (Fig. 8)

8. To store the Polarfleece poncho, cut and sew a separate bag. Cut two pieces of fabric 16" x 22". Sew them together around three sides with right sides facing and hem the open edge. Fold the poncho in thirds and bring it together to slide into the bag. This makes a great pillow for the car when you're not wearing the poncho.

Options:
* Sew Velcro tabs on each open side of the poncho to hold it closed on a windy day.
* Make the poncho from shiny black nylon fabric for an evening wear poncho.

This poncho, in nylon fabrics, folds very compactly to fit into a suitcase or briefcase. It will serve as a windbreaker at a fall football game and spread flat, it's a great ground cover for a picnic.

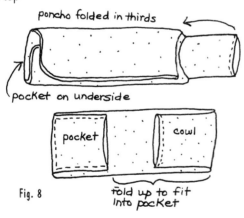

Fig. 8

Rita's Ruana

Throw this wrap over your shoulders to stay warm outdoors or while traveling or watching television. It's easy to sew and wear and there are no fitting problems with this project! Rita Farro has been sharing this fun, warm wrap at her seminars and in her book. That's how it got its name. She likes to add fake-fur binding to the edges of her ruanas.

Joan's out of her rocking chair and ready for a shopping trip in this red Polarfleece version of Rita's Ruana. Purple knit trim covers the edges of the ruana. This wrap is quick to sew and to put on when you need a little warmth. Joan says it's also a great wrap for staying cozy while sitting in the rocker and watching television. Polarfleece by Malden Mills.

Supply List:
2 yds. Polarfleece, wool, or heavy knit fabric, 54" wide or wider
1 yd. knit fabric for trim

1. Cut off one selvedge edge from the ruana fabric. Fold the fabric in half lengthwise, adjusting the foldline to 27" wide. Trim off the extra strip of fabric. (Fig. 1)

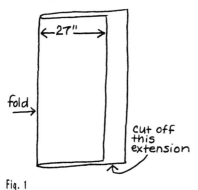

Fig. 1

Mark the shoulder line at 36". Then mark 2" from the fold, starting at the bottom edge and marking all the way to the shoulder line. Cut along the marks and round out the neck opening. (Fig. 2)

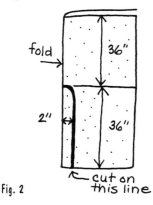

Fig. 2

Also round out all the square corners to make it easier to sew the trim to the ruana. (Fig. 3)

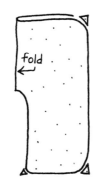

Fig. 3

2. Try on the ruana to test its length and width. Cut smaller if necessary. At this point you can wear the ruana as it is, if the fabric you've chosen is non-fray such as Polarfleece.

3. There are options for finishing the edge on Polarfleece. One is the edge stitch which creates a scalloped edge, as described in the scarf project on page 41. (Fig. 4)

Fig. 4

Another choice is to bind all the edges, as I did on the red ruana. You will need approximately nine yards (324") of binding. Cut the trim strips 4" wide and across the grain of the fabric. To sew the strips together for the binding, place the ends of the strips perpendicular to each and sew diagonally across. (Fig. 5)

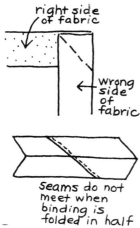

Fig. 5

Trim the seam allowances and press flat. This seaming method will eliminate layers of bulk when the binding is folded and attached to the ruana.

4. Prepare the edges of the Polarfleece ruana by serging all the way around. This process flattens the fabric edge and makes it easier to sew on the binding. Fold the trim strip in half lengthwise, wrong sides together, and press. Sew to the edge of the right side of the ruana with the raw edges meeting the serged edges. Use a 1/4" seam allowance. Turn the folded edge of the binding to the wrong side of the ruana and pin over the seam. (Fig. 6) Stitch in the ditch from the right side of the ruana to attach the back of the binding.

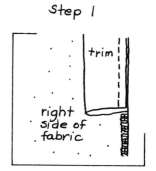

Fig. 6

Options:
* Skip the binding and cut fringe in the bottom edges of the ruana; it's a quick no-sew effect.

This casual wrap is easy to make, comfortable to wear as a light wrap, and adds a little style to your appearance as you dash to the grocery store.

Travel & Television Shawl

This multiple-use shawl has lots of great features: hidden cuffs to slide your arms through to keep the shawl on, pockets for storage or keeping your hands warm, and a great way to fold up and store the shawl in the form of a small pillow.

In the car or at home, the Travel & Television Shawl keeps Dorothy comfortable. The pockets on the front of the shawl keep hands warm or store supplies. The edges of the Polarfleece shawl are wrapped with black elastic wrap trim. Polarfleece by Malden Mills.

Thanks to sleeve cuffs inside the shawl, Dorothy doesn't have to worry that the shawl will slide off when she stands and walks. Inserting her arms through the cuffs also makes the shawl drape gracefully as she wears it.

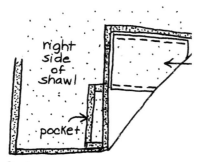

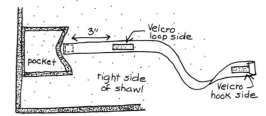

Supply List:

2 yds. Polarfleece, 60" wide (2 yds. will make two shawls)

8 yds. binding (I used elastic binding)

30" ribbon, 1-1/2" wide

3" strip Velcro, 3/4" wide

flat button and 1-1/2" Ultrasuede square for front closure

1. Cut a piece of Polarfleece 22" wide and 72" long. (Change the measurements to fit your needs or preferences.) If you have only one yard of Polarfleece, you can piece the shawl with a seamline in the center back.

2. Sew around the edge of the shawl with an edge stitch to form a scalloped edge (see scarf project on page 41) or bind the edges. I find that serging the edges first flattens the fabric and makes it easier to wrap and sew the binding around the edges.

3. Cut two pockets for the front of the shawl. I made the pockets 8" wide and 9" tall, but these measurements can be changed. Edge stitch or bind the pocket edges as you did with the shawl edges. Sew the pockets to the ends of the shawl, centering them. (Fig. 1)

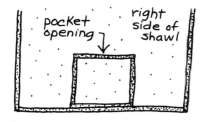

Fig. 1

4. To add the inside "cuffs" which allow you to slide the shawl onto your arms and hold it on more easily, cut two pieces of Polarfleece 7" x 9". Sew them on the wrong side of the front corners of the shawl, sewing down both 9" edges. (Fig. 2)

Fig. 2

Try the shawl on to test the size of the cuffs on your arms. Sew them narrower if you want a tighter fit.

5. For another closure option, sew a 1-1/2" tab of Ultrasuede approximately 20" from the front bottom edge and inside the shawl's front edge. Cut a vertical opening in the tab to fit the button, which you will sew inside the opposite side of the shawl. This closure is another way to prevent the shawl from sliding off while you are wearing it. (Fig. 3)

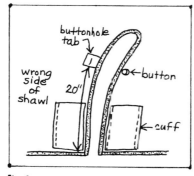

Fig. 3

6. To make the shawl compact and convenient for travel, sew one end of a 30" piece of ribbon onto the shawl inside one of the pockets. Measure 3" from the sewn-down end of the ribbon and sew on the loop (soft) side of a 3" piece of Velcro. At the opposite end of the ribbon and on the other side, turn under the ribbon edge and sew the hook (rough) side of the Velcro. (Fig. 4)

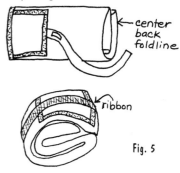

Fig. 4

Now you can fold the shawl in half on the center back line, fold in the sides to the pocket edges, and roll it up. (Fig. 5) The ribbon with the Velcro will hold the shawl together in a neat and compact package.

Fig. 5

Keep this shawl handy near the television and also in the car. In its wrapped up form, it will work as a small pillow also.

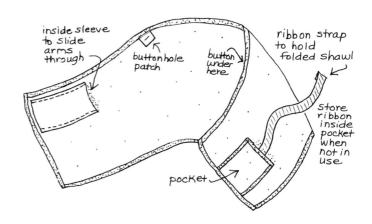

Fringed Shawl

According to my research, shawl sizes vary from 60" to 85" in length and 22" to 28" in width. The best way to determine the length that's right for you is to wrap a two-yard piece of fabric around yourself, first folding it to a 22" width. If the size feels comfortable, use the measurements for your own shawl. In case you don't have enough of one fabric to make a whole shawl, piece it together as I did on the shawl pictured on the left. There's also a different fabric lining the shawl and on the end of the lining on one side, I've added a pocket for a small hidden storage place.

Yarn fringe at the ends of this shawl complements the colors of this wool jersey shawl and its dusty lavender lining. With a button and loop closure, the corner ends of the shawl wrap around Elsie's wrists, keeping the shawl in place. She's standing near the door of my home with the colorful petunias in the window box. I took extra-good care of the flowers in advance of the photo session.

Lorraine's ready for an evening at the symphony in her bright shawl with its cord fringe, quick and easy to sew to the ends of the shawl. See the detail photo of the button and loop closure that keeps this slippery fabric shawl in place while she moves and walks.

Add a loop to the front edge bottom corners of the shawl and sew buttons to the inside bottom edge. Now the shawl has a loop end to slide your hand and arm through. This little detail keeps the shawl on your body and creates a beautiful drape as you wear it.

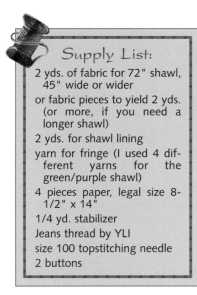

Supply List:

2 yds. of fabric for 72" shawl, 45" wide or wider

or fabric pieces to yield 2 yds. (or more, if you need a longer shawl)

2 yds. for shawl lining

yarn for fringe (I used 4 different yarns for the green/purple shawl)

4 pieces paper, legal size 8-1/2" x 14"

1/4 yd. stabilizer

Jeans thread by YLI

size 100 topstitching needle

2 buttons

1. After determining your best shawl size, cut the fabric and lining to that size.

2. If piecing the fabric as I did, plan the divisions and allow for seams. Sew the sections together with a 1/2" seam allowance and press the seams open. For added detail at the seamlines, I used Jeans thread to sew a decorative stitch between the two fabrics. (Fig. 1)

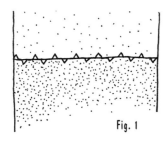

Fig. 1

I chose lavender thread to coordinate with the color of the lining fabric. Practice with scraps of fabric to select the stitch you like best. Place a strip of removable stabilizer under each seamline. (I used Totally Stable by Sulky and temporarily fused it on.) Sew across all seamlines and remove the stabilizer.

3. If you want to add fringe, this is the time to make it. Fold two pieces of legal size paper in half so they measure 14" x 4-1/4". Tape the ends together, overlapping 1" as shown. (Fig. 2)

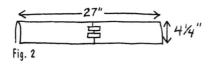

Fig. 2

Knot the yarns you've chosen together and pin the knot to the paper at one end. Loosely wrap the yarns around the paper. You can leave spaces for less full fringe. Now stitch across one long edge of the paper, 1/2" from the edge. (Fig. 3)

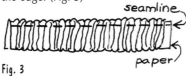

seamline

paper

Fig. 3

Pin the paper and the yarn to the right side of the end of the shawl, as shown, and sew along the line again to anchor the yarn. Sew twice across the paper or use a reinforced stitch. (Fig. 4)

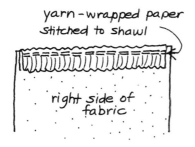

yarn-wrapped paper stitched to shawl

right side of fabric

Fig. 4

Cut the loops at the bottom and top of the paper. Carefully pull away the wide piece of paper first, then the narrow piece at the top edge of the fringe. For the pink shawl, I cut narrow satin braid in 5" pieces and spaced them 1-1/2" apart across the end of the shawl and sewed them to the fabric.

4. Sewing a pocket to the shawl lining is a nice addition. This pocket offers a hidden storage spot for tissue, keys, or money when you are wearing or using the shawl. The finished size of the pocket I added is 8-1/2" x 5". A small piece of Velcro under the top edge holds the pocket closed and keeps the contents inside. (Fig. 5)

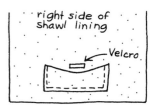

right side of shawl lining

Velcro

Fig. 5

5. Pin the shawl front and lining together with the right sides facing. Pin all the edges, using plenty of pins, especially if your fabrics are fluid and soft and shift easily. Sew from the wrong side of the shawl front and keep the fringe out of the seamlines along the sides. Leave an opening to pull the shawl right side out. Trim and press the seam, then turn the shawl right side out. Finally, press the shawl edges to flatten them. Sew the opening on the seamline for a gap-free seamline when you wear the shawl.

6. I watched a movie in which an actress wore a shawl with the bottom corners wrapped to form sleeves. I call this the "movie star feature." Wrap the end of the shawl around your wrist and mark the place where the corner meets the edge of the shawl. Sew a small flat button to the bottom edge of the shawl lining near the top of the fringe. Make a loop from two pieces of the fringe, or sew a loop to the edge of the shawl. (Fig. 6)

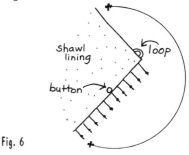

shawl lining

loop

button

Fig. 6

...secrets of a smart shawl...

pocket sewn to shawl lining for secret storage place

Button and loop to wrap shawl around wrist

Commuter Bib

The response to this car bib for adults has been very positive. It makes great sense to cover your clothing while dining on the road. The bib stores in its own pocket to make a small car pillow when you're not eating. It's also a dignified clothing cover for a nursing home resident.

Like so many of us who eat in our cars, Joan's ready to dine, protecting her clothes with the Commuter Bib. The fabric yoke is sewn to a bath towel and wraps around the neck so the bib stays in place. Yoke fabric by Hoffman.

Supply List:

bath towel
2/3 yd. fabric for yoke and pocket, 45" wide or wider
5" strip Velcro, 3/4" wide
Optional:
    lining fabric for towel, for more dining protection

1. On the tissue pattern sheets, locate the yoke for the Commuter Bib and cut two from fabric.

2. With right sides facing, sew the two fabric yokes together using a 1/4" seam allowance and leaving the bottom edge open. (Fig. 1)

wrong side of fabric

Fig. 1

Clip and trim the seam allowances, press, and turn the yoke right side out. Press all the edges of the yoke. Turn the open bottom edges under 1/4" and press. (Fig. 2)

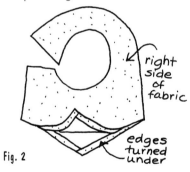

right side of fabric

edges turned under

Fig. 2

3. Fold the top edges of the towel to fit inside the yoke, as illustrated. (Fig. 3)

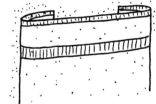

Fig. 3

Pin the towel to the inside back of the yoke and sew to attach it there. (Fig. 4) Trim away some of the towel above the seamline to reduce bulk.

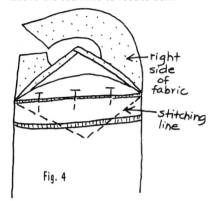

right side of fabric

stitching line

Fig. 4

4. Pin the top yoke edge over the seamline and sew to secure the yoke front to the towel.

5. Try on the bib to determine the amount of overlap needed on the bib strap. Remember that the bib will be worn over clothing and/or coats. Mark both the strap and the yoke at the point of intersection. Sew the Velcro to the bib front and under the flap. (Fig. 5)

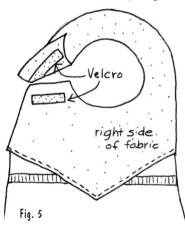

Velcro

right side of fabric

Fig. 5

6. Make a pocket for storing the bib. Fold the towel in half lengthwise and measure the width. Cut the pocket fabric 1" wider and 10-12" tall. Turn under and press the edges of the pocket piece. Sew the pocket to the towel with the pocket opening at the bottom of the towel (it can be sewn to the bib front or back - it's your choice). (Fig. 6)

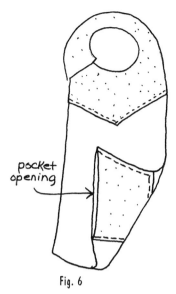

pocket opening

Fig. 6

7. Fold the towel in half lengthwise, then fold the pocket portion toward the center. Fold the towel and yoke top down and fold and roll into the pocket. (Fig. 7)

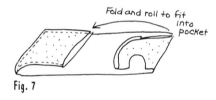

Fold and roll to fit into pocket

Fig. 7

Make this bib as a gift for men and women. They're sure to report that they use it and that it has saved their clothing from food spills.

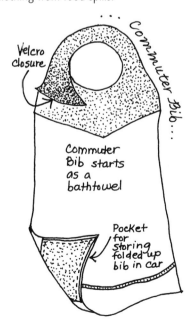

Commuter Bib...

Velcro closure

Commuter Bib starts as a bathtowel

Pocket for storing folded-up bib in car

Golf Shoe Bag

Pack your golf shoes in this carrier decorated with an appropriate applique and featuring a zipper pocket on the back, just right for keys, money, or other small items.

Store golf or other shoes in this two-pocket bag. A golf ball applique trims one of the pockets and on the back of the bag is a zipper pocket for holding money, golf tees, or other supplies. The little viola flowers are in a garden area under a tree in the front of my home.

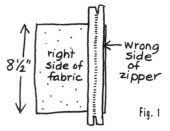

Supply List:
1/2 yd. canvas/duck fabric, 45" wide or wider
20" webbing for bag handle
9" or longer zipper
Ultrasuede scraps for applique
paper-backed fusible web or spray fusible for applique
small piece of stabilizer

1. Cut one piece of fabric 8-1/2" x 30" for the back of the shoe bag. Cut two pieces 8-1/2" x 14" for the shoe pockets. Cut one piece 8-1/2" x 6-1/2" for the zipper pocket.

2. Make the zipper pocket on the back of the bag first. With the right side of the zipper lined up with and facing the right side of one 8-1/2" edge of the zipper pocket piece, stitch the zipper to the fabric. (Fig. 1)

8½"

right side of fabric

wrong side of zipper

Fig. 1

Press the seam, then topstitch near the edge of the zipper. (Fig. 2)

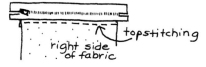

Fig. 2

Pin the pocket piece with the zipper attached 6" from one end of the bag back with the right sides of the fabric facing and the zipper at the 6" mark. (Fig. 3)

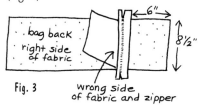

Fig. 3

Sew the long edge of the zipper to the bag back, turn the zipper and pocket down, and press. Sew across the ends of the zipper, remembering to pull the zipper head inside the seam-line. Sew or baste the pocket sides and bottom to the bag back. (Fig. 4)

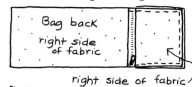

Fig. 4

3. Add the applique to one or both of the shoe pocket fronts at this time. Also consider a monogram. To speed the process, I chose Ultrasuede for each of the shapes. In my stash of Ultrasuede, I have a white perforated variety which is perfect to represent a golf ball. If you are using solid non-fray fabric, consider adding a few holes with an eyelet punch to suggest the dimpled surface of a golf ball. (Fig. 5) Use paper-backed fusible web or spray fusible to attach

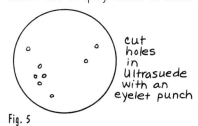

cut holes in Ultrasuede with an eyelet punch

Fig. 5

the shapes to the pocket front. Add stabilizer under the fabric and stitch around the edges of the shapes with a narrow zigzag stitch and clear thread. Remove the stabilizer after stitching.

4. At the top edge of each shoe pocket piece, turn the edge under twice and sew it down.

5. Mark the center point along each side of the bag back. Then mark points 2-1/2" on either side of the center points. On this 5" edge on each side of the bag back, turn the edges under twice toward the wrong side of the bag back and stitch it down. (Fig. 6)

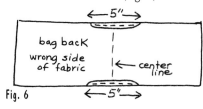

Fig. 6

6. Pin the pocket pieces on the bag back with the right sides of the fabric facing and the top edges of the pockets closest to the center line. Sew twice around the bottom and sides of each pocket, using a 1/2" seam allowance.

(Fig. 7) Serge or trim the seam allowances and turn the bag right side out and press.

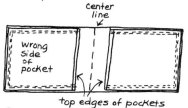

Fig. 7

7. Wrap the webbing around the center of the bag and overlap it 2". Pin the overlap on the back side of the bag. Sew the webbing to the back of the bag along the edges of the strap, creating a handle on the top. (Fig. 8)

Fig. 8

This bag will fit golf shoes for men and women. It's a great gift for a golfer. Use it for other kinds of shoes too.

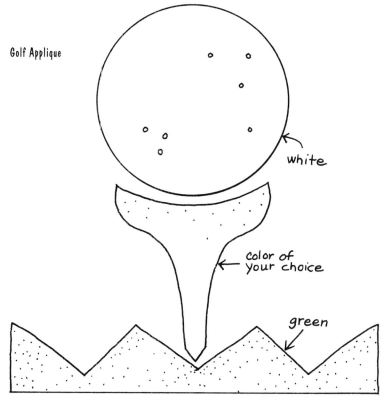

Golf Applique

white

Color of your choice

green

Golfer's Purse

Carry the necessities in this bag trimmed with spare golf tees and featuring a key ring to attach to a golf bag. Make it to match the golf shoe bag for a coordinated set.

A colorful Golfer's Purse conveniently hangs from a golf bag. It features an elastic strip holding golf tees and two zipper compartments. This project is a perfect gift for a golfing friend.

Supply List:

- 1/4 yd. canvas fabric, 45" wide or wider
- 1/8 yd. for contrasting fabric
- 10" zipper for top of bag
- 4" or longer zipper for front pocket
- 4" strip of 3/8" clear elastic for golf tee holder
- 1/4 yd. fabric for bag lining, 45" wide or wider
- "D" ring or key ring

1. Cut the sections of the bag from fabric. Cut two pieces 10" x 2-1/2" for the bag top section and two pieces 10" x 5-1/2" for the bag bottom section. Cut two pieces of bag lining fabric 10" x 7-1/2".

2. Cut a strip of fabric as wide as the zipper and 6" long. Sew the right side of it to the right side of the bag front zipper, placing the fabric 3-1/2" from the top of the zipper. (Fig. 1)

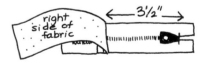

Fig. 1

Turn the strip down over the bottom of the zipper and trim away the excess zipper length. Cut one bag bottom fabric into two pieces as shown. (Fig. 2)

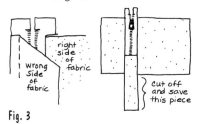

Fig. 2

Sew the zipper to the 5-1/2" edges of the two sections of the bag bottom, with the right side of the zipper piece facing the right sides of the bottom sections. (Fig. 3)

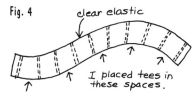

Fig. 3

Press the seams. Cut off the extra narrow strip extending beyond the bottom of the bag and save it to use with the zipper at the top of the bag.

3. To decorate the bag with golf tees, sew the elastic strip to the purse front. A curving line is more interesting than a straight one. Sew vertical lines through the elastic 1/4" apart. I sewed ten double-stitched vertical lines and placed tees in every other space. (Fig. 4)

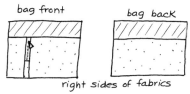

Fig. 4

clear elastic

I placed tees in these spaces.

4. Sew the zipper section to one top section of the bag. Sew the other bottom and top sections together to create the back of the bag. (Fig. 5)

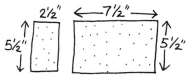

bag front   bag back

right sides of fabrics

Fig. 5

5. Prepare the zipper for the bag top. Find that leftover fabric strip from Step

2 and cut it in half. Sew each half over the ends of the zipper so it is now 3/4" shorter on each end. (Fig. 6)

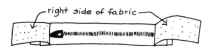

right side of fabric

Fig. 6

Trim away the excess zipper ends. The fabric tab on each end of the zipper reduces the bulk at the bag corners so neater corners can be turned out when the bag is sewn together.

6. Pin and sew one edge of the zipper to the bag front. The zipper's right side will meet the fabric's right side. Pin the bag lining top edge, right side down, to the zipper edge you just stitched, sandwiching the zipper between the two layers of fabric. (Fig. 7)

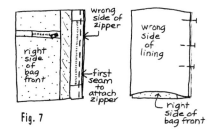

wrong side of zipper

right side of bag front

first seam to attach zipper

wrong side of lining

right side of bag front

Fig. 7

Stitch the lining to the zipper by following the stitching you just finished. Follow the same procedure to sew the opposite side of the zipper to the bag back and lining. Turn the lining fabrics so they are inside the bag.

7. To make the pocket on the front of the bag, draw a line extending 5" beyond the bottom of the front pocket zipper and 3-1/2" up to the edge of the bag top section. Sew through the front bag and lining fabrics along the

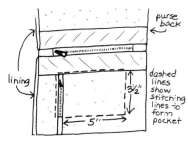

purse back

lining

dashed lines show stitching lines to form pocket

3½"

5"

Fig. 8

lines, along the bottom edge of the top section, and along the left side of the zipper. (Fig. 8) Now there's a pocket on the front of the purse.

8. Cut a fabric or ribbon strip 2" long for a key ring or an attachment to hook the purse to a golf bag. Fold the strip in half, insert a "D" ring or a key ring and pin the strip to the side seam on the bag front. (Fig. 9)

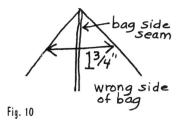

D ring or Key ring

Bag front

Fig. 9

9. With the bag's right sides together, pin and sew the bag and bag lining together at the side and bottom. Reinforce the stitching over the fabric loop on the side of the bag.

10. To form a bottom to the bag, form a triangle by bringing together the seamlines of the bag bottom and sides, as described in the Techniques section on page 7. Measure and mark a line 1-3/4" across and sew this line on each corner. (Fig. 10)

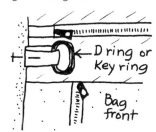

bag side seam

1¾"

wrong side of bag

Fig. 10

Turn the bag right side out and push out the corners. Press. Add zipper pulls to each zipper for ease in opening and closing

If you skip the golf tee decoration, this small purse could be a useful bag for everyday use. Consider a monogram as a decoration, using the alphabet letters on page 93.

Golf Brim Hat

Make this smart brimmed visor for your favorite golfer. The headband is adjustable and also features a removable and washable sweatband, a very smart addition. This hat, along with the Gardener's Hat on page 62, was designed by Carolyn McCormick.

Helen's ready for a golf date in her bright pink Golf Brim Hat. Her eyes will be shaded by the Timtex-lined brim and the back of the hat adjusts with a Velcro closure. Hat fabric by P & B Fabrics.

The pink flannel strip forming the removable sweatband is attached inside the hat band with Velcro.

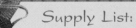

Supply List:

1 yd. fabric, 45" wide or wider

1/2 yd. fabric for contrasting lower brim

2" x 28" strip flannel, stretch terrycloth, or other absorbent natural fabric

28" strip Velcro, 3/4" wide

1 yd. fusible interfacing or Timtex (13" x 12") for hat brim

1. On the tissue pattern sheets, locate the pieces for the Golf Brim Hat and the Hat Band. Cut from fabric as directed on the pattern pieces. Also cut a piece of flannel 2" x 28" for the sweatband.

2. Fold and press the hat band in half lengthwise with the wrong sides of the fabric together. Open up the band and sew the loop (soft) side of the Velcro to the right side of the fabric, 1/2" below the fold, sewing only on the top edge of the Velcro. (Fig. 1)

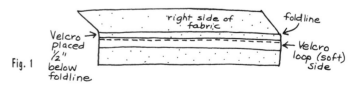

Fig. 1

Baste the two layers of the band together, stitching next to but not on the bottom edge of the Velcro.

3. Cut and fuse interfacing to the wrong side of each layer of the brim. Use two layers if you prefer a stiffer brim. Place the right sides of the brim together and sew around the outside edge with a 1/4" seam allowance. Turn right side out and press. Add a row of topstitching around the edge. If you use Timtex, a hat brim product, sew the two brim fabrics together first (no interfacing added). Using the brim pattern, make a tracing of the brim on Timtex. Then cut the brim piece 1/4" to 1/2" smaller than the pattern. Attach the Timtex to the wrong side of one of the brim layers with pieces of paper-backed fusible web. (Fig. 2)

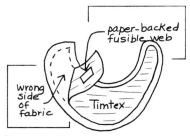

Fig. 2

Then turn the brim right side out and sew a row of topstitching 1/2" from the edge of the brim and through all the layers of fabric and Timtex.

4. Baste along the inside edge of the brim through all the layers with very narrow seam allowances (less than 1/4"). Next you will sew the band to the brim with right sides together and a 1/4" seam allowance. To do this, place the brim down on the sewing machine and the band on top with the Velcro strip facing up and the raw edges of the band aligned with the raw edges of the brim. (Fig. 3)

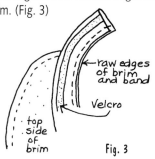

Fig. 3

Sew from the center of the brim out to each end, stretching the brim gently to straighten it as you sew it to the band. Slide the seam allowances under the loose edge of the Velcro on the band and sew from the outside band, using the basting line sewn previously as a guide. Stitch slightly above the basting. (Fig. 4)

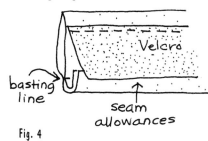

Fig. 4

5. Try on the hat to test the length and overlap of the band. Cut the bands shorter if the overlap is excessive. Serge or zigzag the raw ends of the band and sew a 2" strip of the hook (rough) side of Velcro to the left outside of the band. (Fig. 5)

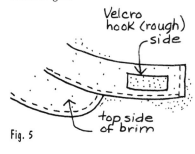

Fig. 5

With the band held together with the Velcro, measure the band inside to determine the length of the sweatband. (Fig. 6)

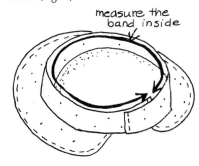

Fig. 6

6. To make the removable sweatband, cut the strip of flannel to the band measurement and press in the long edges with the wrong sides together. Sew a strip of the hook (rough) side of Velcro in the center of the flannel and over the fabric raw edges. (Fig. 7)

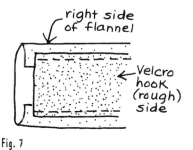

Fig. 7

Attach the sweatband inside the hat band and you're ready to wear the hat for a golf day or anytime you need a brimmed hat. Remove and wash the sweatband after a strenuous day on the golf course. That way, you won't have to clean the hat as often.

This visor-type hat will shade your eyes on the golf course or wherever you travel. To learn how to add a crown or top to this brim, read the instructions for the Gardener's Hat on the next page.

Gardener's Hat

This hat is the first of four accessories made from one gardening-themed tablecloth. Like the golf brim hat on the preceding pages, it has a removable sweatband. This hat is also adjustable so you can make it snug on your head on a windy day and it has a vented opening in the back to help you stay cool. It's fun to make the bottom brim of a different fabric for a little contrast. Carolyn McCormick designed this hat as well as the Golf Brim Hat.

Nancy takes a break from her flower gardening to show off the Gardener's Hat. Details include the green piping around the edge of the brim and a second fabric selected for the inside of the brim. The top of the brim and the hat crown are made from a gardening theme tablecloth. Brim lining fabric by Hoffman.

The Gardener's Hat has an overlapping brim and the back of the hat is open for ventilation. Like the Golf Brim Hat on page 60, this hat also has a removable sweatband and is adjustable, thanks to the Velcro closure.

Supply List:

1 yd. fabric, 45" wide or wider (or tablecloth)
5/8 yd. fabric for brim lining
28" strip Velcro, 3/4" wide
1 yd. fusible interfacing or 18" square of Timtex
1/2 yd. lightweight fusible interfacing for hat top and crown

2" x 28" strip flannel, stretch terrycloth, or other absorbent, natural fabric
Optional:
    50" piping for edge of brim

1. On the tissue pattern sheets, locate the pieces for the Gardener's Hat Crown Top, Gardener's Hat Brim, Gardener's Hat Crown, and the Hat Band. (Notice that there are options for the size of the back of the brim. The hat shown here uses the larger brim to protect the wearer's neck from the sun.) Using the fabrics chosen for this project, follow Steps 1-6 of the instructions for the Golf Brim Hat on the preceding pages. Try the hat brim around your head. If it overlaps many inches, consider adjusting the brim size as well as the hat crown and crown top. If you add the piping to the edge of the hat brim, sew it to the top brim before sewing on the lower brim. Follow the stitching line for attaching the piping when you sew the upper and lower brim fabrics together.

2. Cut the hat crown and crown top from both the hat and lining fabrics. Fuse interfacing to the wrong sides of the crown and crown top fashion fabric. Sew the short ends of the crown strip together with the right sides of the fabric meeting and a 1/4" seam allowance. (Fig. 1)

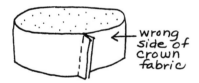

Fig. 1

3. Sew the crown side to the crown top with the right sides together and matching front, back, and middle points of each piece. (Fig. 2)

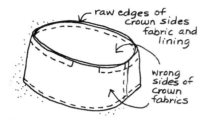

Fig. 2

Use a 1/4" seam allowance. Repeat these steps for the two pieces of the crown lining.

4. Pin the right sides of the crown and lining together, using a 1/4" seam allowance to sew around and leaving an opening so you can turn the crown right side out. (Fig. 3)

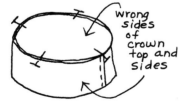

Fig. 3

Turn under and press the crown edge and edge stitch around the entire bottom edge.

5. Place the crown on top of the hat brim, just as it will appear when finished. Sew the crown to the hat band, sewing around the front from ear to ear and leaving the back half of the crown unsewn. (Fig. 4)

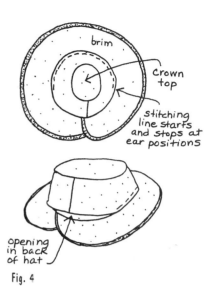

Fig. 4

6. Adjust the band to fit your head and pull the crown down over the band.

Enjoy gardening in this practical and attractive hat. The brim protects your face and neck and the opening in the back of the crown ventilates your head. When the wind starts to blow, tighten the band so you don't lose your hat.

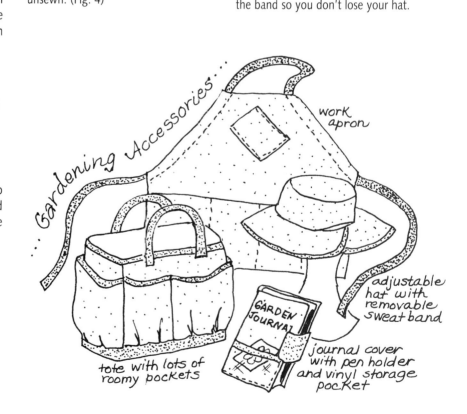

Gardening Accessories

work apron

tote with lots of roomy pockets

GARDEN JOURNAL

adjustable hat with removable sweat band

journal cover with pen holder and vinyl storage pocket

Gardener's Work Apron

This apron is quick to sew and handy to wear for work projects in the garden or your home. Size the pockets to fit your equipment, add a loop for hanging the apron in a handy spot, and thread ribbon through the casings to form the apron ties and neck strap. This project was also made from the gardening tablecloth mentioned in the Gardener's Hat project.

Get set for spade work with this apron, made from a gardening theme tablecloth. The top front pocket is sewn on at an angle for easy access to sunglasses or a garden tool. The row of pockets across the bottom holds seed packages and lots of other supplies. The ribbon that forms the neck loop slides through side casings to make the apron ties. This scene is in a garden area in the backyard of my home.

Supply List:

1 yd. sturdy fabric, 45" wide or wider (or a tablecloth)

3 yds. ribbon, twill tape, or other strapping for apron ties and neck strap

1. On the tissue pattern sheets, locate the piece for the Gardener's Work Apron. To make the apron narrower or wider, move the pattern piece over or away from the foldline. Cut the apron body from fabric. Also cut fabric 8-1/2" x 30" for the pocket section at the bottom of the apron, a 7" x 9" piece for top pocket, and a strip 1-3/4" x 8" for the hanging loop at the top edge of the apron.

2. Serge the top edge of each pocket piece or turn under twice and sew. Then turn under each top edge once again and sew it to the pocket. (Fig. 1)

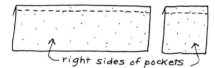

Fig. 1

3. Place the right side of the bottom pocket section to the wrong side of the apron, pinning across the bottom. (Fig. 2)

Fig. 2

Sew the bottom edge with 1/4" seam allowances, press the seam, and bring the pocket section to the right side of the apron. Pin in place on the apron.

4. Serge or zigzag all the raw edges of the apron. Turn under the sides and top edge (not the diagonal edges) and sew in place. (Fig. 3)

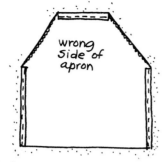

Fig. 3

5. On the right side of the apron, mark 1-3/4" from the diagonal edges. Turn under on the lines and sew the fabric edges in place, using a double or reinforced seam. (Fig. 4) This stitching forms the casings that the apron cord will pass through.

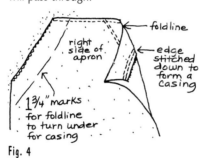

Fig. 4

6. Sew divisions in the pocket section at the bottom of the apron. Plan the sizes to fit the supplies you will carry.

7. Turn under the sides of the top pocket, pin, and sew the pocket to the front of the apron in a location convenient for your use. I placed the pocket at a slant for easy access (for a right-handed person) to gloves or sunglasses.

8. Fold the fabric strip for the hanging loop in half lengthwise with right sides facing and stitch with 1/4" seam allowances. Turn right side out. At the top of the apron, turn the ends of the strip over the apron edge and stitch the loop securely in place. This loop will hold a towel or provide a way to hang the apron when you're not wearing it. (Fig. 5)

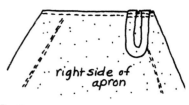

Fig. 5

9. Thread the ribbon or cord through the side casings. When you wear the apron, you can adjust the length of the neck strap for your own comfort. (Fig. 6)

Fig. 6

This apron would be fine as a sewing and craft apron. Make the bottom row of pockets with clear vinyl so you can see what you're carrying. It's easily adapted for many different uses and protects your clothing while you're at work.

Garden Tote

Here's another project made from the garden tablecloth. This tote has a reinforced bottom, dark fabric handles and trim, and lots of pockets for gardening tools and supplies. Have everything you need on hand as you dig in the dirt.

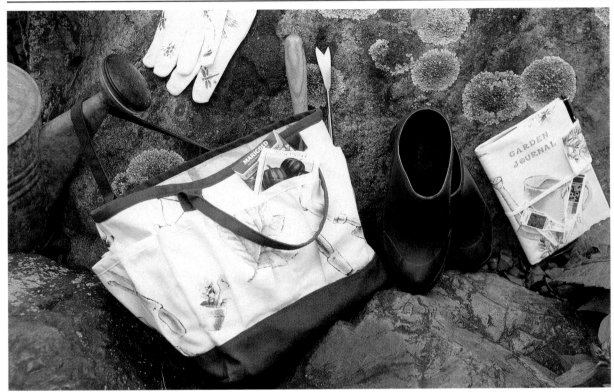

The gardening theme tablecloth was also used for this tote bag with its row of pockets surrounding the bag. The bottom is reinforced with a solid green fabric and the top edge is bound with the same fabric. This bag will hold gardening tools and supplies and even your cell phone while you spend time with the weeds and seeds. The gloves were stenciled with Diane Ericson's "Bug" stencils (see Resources, page 96) to coordinate with the gardening motif. I still use the old-fashioned watering can you see in the photo.

Supply List:

- 1 yd. duck canvas or other durable fabric, 45" wide or wider (or a tablecloth)
- 1/2 yd. durable fabric for contrasting trim, reinforced bag bottom, and handles
- 1 yd. crisp fusible interfacing
- 1 pkg. extra-wide double-fold bias tape

1. Cut the following pieces for the bag and pockets:

from print fabric or tablecloth
- 1 piece 28" x 13" for bag front, bottom, and back
- 2 pieces 11" x 6" for bag sides
- 2 pieces 17" x 7" for pockets (front and back)
- 2 pieces 7" x 8" for side pockets

from contrasting fabric
- 1 piece 11" x 13" for bag bottom reinforcement
- 2 pieces 2-1/2" x 6" for bag side reinforcements
- 2 pieces 3" x 18" for bag handles

2. Cut interfacing for the bag front, bottom, and back piece and for the two side pieces. Fuse it to the wrong sides of these three pieces of fabric.

3. Sew bias binding to the top edge of the four pocket pieces. Pin each pocket section 2-1/2" from the top edge of the bag piece or the bag side, meeting the pocket sides to the bag side edges. (Fig. 1)

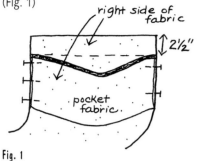

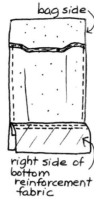

Fig. 1

Since the pocket sections are wider than the bag, each pocket will have extra room. Sew the pocket sides to the bag pieces with a 1/4" seam allowance. Plan the number of pocket sections you will sew on the bag front and back. Pin the pleats into the bottom edges of each pocket section you are planning. (Fig. 2)

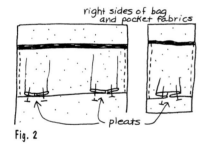

Fig. 2

Sew across the bottoms of the pockets on the back, front, and sides of the bag with 1/4" seam allowances. Sew the vertical division lines in the pocket sections on the bag front and back.

4. Press under 1/4" on the 13" edges of the bag bottom reinforcement fabric. Place the piece wrong side down over the middle of the right side of the bag front and back piece, covering the raw edges of the pockets. (Fig. 3)

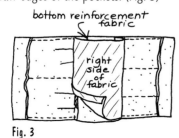

Fig. 3

Pin and sew into place, using a reinforced seam or a double row of stitching.

On the bag side reinforcement pieces, turn under and press 1/4" on one 6" edge. Pin the folded edge over the bottom edge of the pocket section on each bag side piece and sew, again using a reinforced seam or double row of stitching (Fig. 4)

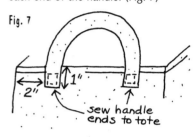

Fig. 4

5. Now it's time to assemble the bag. With right sides together, match the pocket top edges, reinforcement edges, and pin the bag front and back to the bag side pieces. Before sewing, check to see that the sewing machine needle is a size that will handle thick layers of fabric. Sew around the bag sides, pivoting at the corners. (Fig. 5)

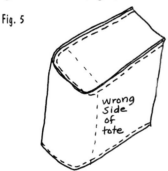

Fig. 5

Add a second seam after checking that the pocket edges lined up with the first stitching and the corners are sewn without pleats in the fabric. (Take out the first stitching and restitch if needed.)

6. Wrap and sew the bag top edge with bias tape or binding cut from the contrasting fabric. You will need approximately 36" of tape or binding.

7. Turn under 1/4" and press the short ends of the bag handle fabrics to the wrong side of the fabric. Then press each long raw edge to the middle where they meet. (Fig. 6)

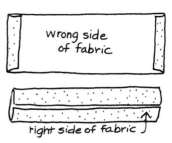

Fig. 6

Position and pin the squared-off ends on the bag front and back 2" from each side seam and 1" below the top binding. Sew a 1" square to anchor each end of the handle. (Fig. 7)

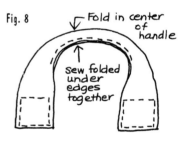

Fig. 7

Fold the rest of the handle in half with the raw edges inside. Sew along the folded under edges. (Fig. 8)

Fig. 8

Options:
* Sew straps with Velcro to attach and hold tools securely in place.

This tote will make it easy to carry your water bottle, hand towel, tools, knee pads, gloves, fertilizer, and cell phone out to the flower bed!

Make sure to label your projects and sign your work. This label, inside the Garden Tote, was decorated with rubber stamps from All Night Media.

Garden Journal Book Cover

Make a gardening record book to match your other garden accessories! Cover your journal with a fabric cover complete with a vinyl pocket for storing seed packages and a fabric closure with Velcro and a loop for your pen.

Keep track of your garden with a special journal, covered with more of the gardening theme tablecloth. A vinyl pocket surrounds the book and holds seed packages or plant markers. A tab closure features a Velcro strip with a space to slide in a pen. I labeled the journal with a set of rubber stamps from All Night Media. Do you recognize the leaf varieties from my garden? There's a rhubarb stalk leaf on the bottom with carrot tops, lettuce leaves, and a cabbage leaf on top.

1. Wrap a tape measure around the front and back of the journal to measure. Also measure the height of the book. Use these two actual measurements as a guide for cutting fabric for the journal cover. (Fig. 1)

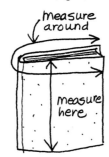

Fig. 1

2. On the right side of the fabric, mark the lines of the journal size using a chalk marker or washable marking pen. Add 3" to each side for the book cover sleeves and add 3/4" to the top and bottom. (Fig. 2) Cut the fabric and serge or zigzag all four edges.

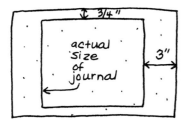

Fig. 2

3. Plan the placement and size of the vinyl pocket. Mine is 4" high and extends from the front to the back. Cut the vinyl and sew a narrow piece of bias binding to the top edge. (For sewing on vinyl, use a Teflon coated presser foot on the sewing machine so the presser foot glides over the vinyl.) Using the lines marking the book's front, back, and bottom edges and tape the vinyl to the book cover at or near the bottom edge. Sew around the sides and bottom edges and sew divisions in the pocket if you wish. (Fig. 3)

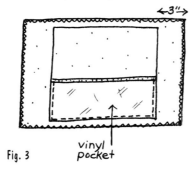

Fig. 3

4. Turn the overlapped edges wrong side out and stitch them in place, with a 3/4" seam allowance, to form the sleeves of the book cover. (Fig. 4)

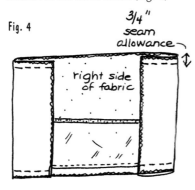

Fig. 4

Turn the sleeves right side out and press the edges, pressing on the wrong side of the book cover. Also press down the serged edges between the sleeves. (Fig. 5) Remember that any pressing you do on the right side of the book cover requires a press cloth over the vinyl!

Fig. 5

5. Cut two pieces of fabric for the tab closure. Mine measured 4" x 3-1/2". Sew the right sides of the fabrics together on three sides, leaving one 3-1/2" edge open. Turn right side out. Turn under the raw edges and pin to the back of the book cover to plan the Velcro placement. (Fig. 6)

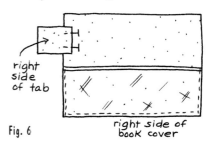

Fig. 6

Sew the loop (soft) side of the Velcro to the tab, leaving a space for a pen to slide in. (Fig. 7)

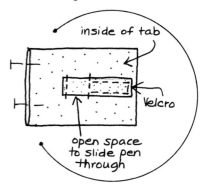

Fig. 7

Sew the pinned end of the tab to the back of the book cover, keeping the sleeve of the book cover out of the stitching area. Sew a smaller piece of the hook side of the Velcro to the journal front.

Label the journal with rubber stamps as I did or with machine embroidery.

Spa Tabi

In less than an hour you can make a pair of spa tabi as a treat for your hard working feet. The spa tabi is a modified version of the tabi, a two-toed cloth foot covering worn in Japan. Apply your favorite foot moisturizer, slide into your spa tabi, put your feet up and relax. This project is designed by Ann Sagawa.

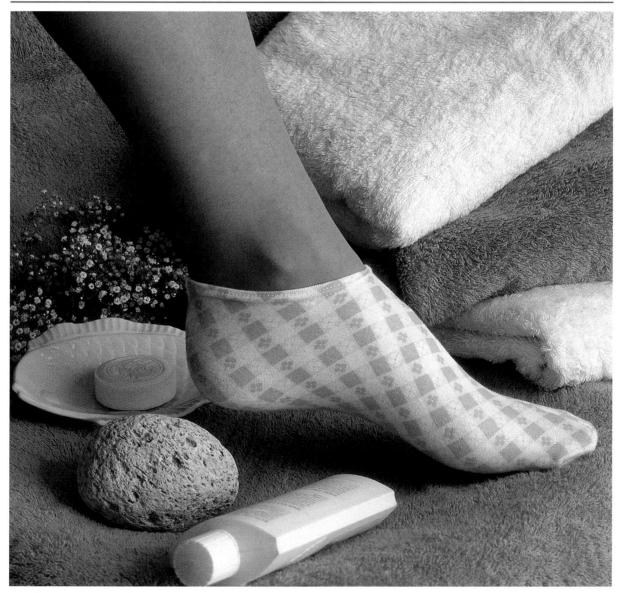

Spread moisturizer on your feet and put on the spa tabi, slipper-type socks to cover your feet while the skin cream does its work. You'll find that sewing the tabi is very quick and easy and they make a wonderful gift, especially paired with the gloves and headband in the following chapters.

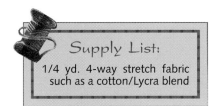

Supply List:

1/4 yd. 4-way stretch fabric such as a cotton/Lycra blend

1. On the tissue pattern sheets, locate the piece for the Spa Tabi. Place the pattern on the fold of the fabric, as illustrated, with the greatest amount of stretch running lengthwise through the pattern. (Fig. 1) Cut two from fabric.

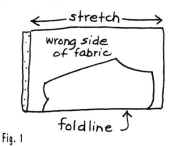

stretch

wrong side of fabric

foldline

Fig. 1

2. Using a serger or sewing machine, sew the center front seam with the right sides of the fabric facing. (Fig. 2) If you are using the sewing machine, use a stretch or narrow zigzag stitch.

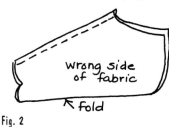

wrong side of fabric

Fold

Fig. 2

3. Match the center toe notch to the center front seam and sew. (Fig. 3)

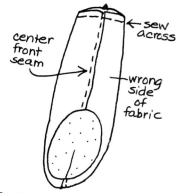

sew across

center front seam

wrong side of fabric

Fig. 3

4. Sew the heel seam. Turn the tabi right side out.
5. Turn the ankle hem down 1/4" and topstitch using a double needle and a stretch or narrow zigzag stitch. (Fig. 4) Repeat on the other tabi.

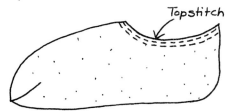

Topstitch

Fig. 4

To custom fit tabi, use these tips:
* If a serged seam in the heel area is uncomfortable, sew the seam with a stretch or zigzag stitch at the sewing machine.
* For a wider foot, increase the height of the center front seam on the pattern piece.
* For a wider ankle, flare out the heel seam on the pattern piece.
* For a longer foot, lengthen the center front seam on the pattern piece.
* Round the toe seam for a better fit.

With its quick and easy seam construction, the spa tabi will be great for last minute gifts or for those who "have everything." Use the same fabric for the other accessories that follow for a coordinated spa gift package.

This kit of spa accessories is sure to be a popular gift. Sew cotton Lycra gloves, headband, and spa tabi from the same fabric, and trim a Pleated Pouch (page 86) with the same fabric. Add a monogram if you like. There's still room for a tube of hand and foot moisturizer, a loofah sponge, or a scented candle to enjoy in a home spa experience.

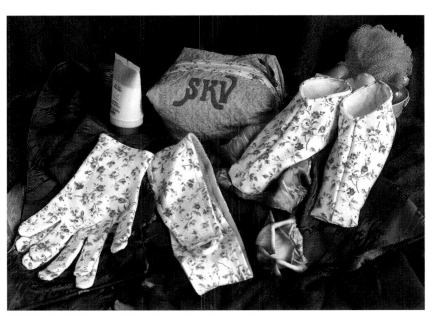

Gloves

Make a pair of gloves from the same fabric chosen for the spa tabi on the previous pages to wear after applying moisturizer to your hands. These gloves can be made for other uses too: for special events such as proms or weddings, for gardening, to coordinate with a special outfit, or for cold weather wear. The sewing is easy and the secret is that you sew the glove outline before you cut out the gloves!

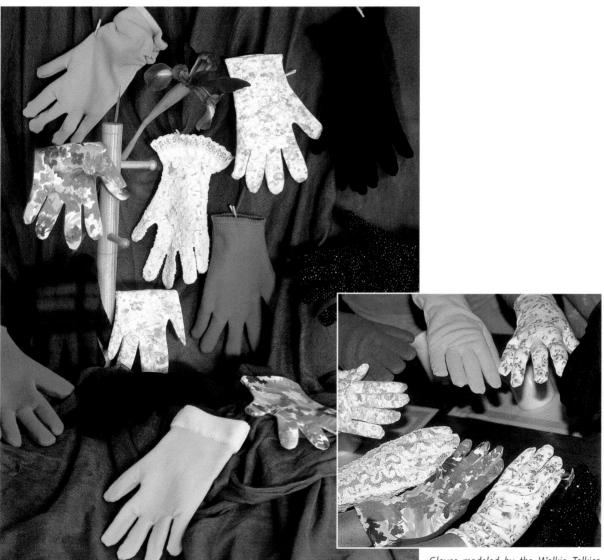

Thanks to Lycra stretch fabrics, gloves are easy to sew. Here you see the variety of styles to consider, from moisturizer or sleep gloves to Polarfleece gloves for warmth to lace gloves for a special evening event. Polarfleece by Malden Mills.

Gloves modeled by the Walkie Talkies, my walking group, at our mid-walk coffee stop at Hank's Bar and Grill in downtown Aurora, Minnesota.

Supply List:

1/3 yd. Lycra blend fabric, 4-way stretch is best
stretch fabric sewing machine needle
polyester thread

1. On the tissue pattern sheets, locate the piece for the Gloves. Two sizes are provided. Start with the size shown with the solid line unless you plan to sew the gloves from a thicker fabric like Polarfleece. Use the dashed line for a larger size. Preserve the tissue pattern by tracing the glove shape on stronger white paper, then carefully cut the glove shape from the paper. The glove outline is the stitching line you'll need to mark and follow on the fabric so it should be as smooth and accurate as possible.

2. Lycra blend fabrics have an amazing amount of stretch so they provide great glove possibilities. Start by tracing one glove on the fabric and sewing it so you can try it on to test the fit. Trace the glove outline on the wrong side of the fabric. Add another piece of fabric beneath the fabric you traced on. (Fig. 1) Make sure you can see the line easily after the pattern is removed. If you cannot easily mark a visible line, pin the paper pattern to the fabric and stitch around the edges.

3. Set the machine for a stretch or repeating stitch and a short stitch length or if you don't have these options, a short stitch length (1.5 or 1.0). (Fig. 2)

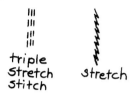

triple
Stretch
Stitch

stretch

Fig. 2

Sew around the outline of the glove, sewing one stitch across the point at the base of the fingers. (Fig. 3)

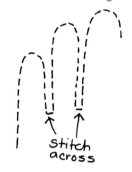

Stitch across

Fig. 3

Try the glove on your hand while the fabric is still wrong sides out and change the stitching lines, if necessary, to improve the fit. Remember that there will be narrow seam allowances

inside the glove when the fabric is turned right side out.

4. Cut the glove from the fabric, leaving a 1/8" seam allowance and clipping carefully into the points where the fingers are stitched. (Fig. 4)

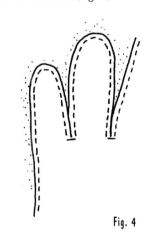

Fig. 4

Turn the glove right side out and press the seamlines to flatten the gloves. Turn under the open end 1/4" and stitch with the same stretch stitch used for the rest of the glove, or use a double needle to sew the hem.

Once you have sewn a pair of gloves and tested the fit, you'll be ready to make more pairs. For options with the glove cuffs, see the illustrations below. (Fig. 5)

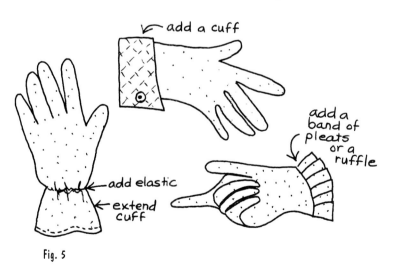

add a cuff

add elastic

extend cuff

add a band of pleats or a ruffle

Fig. 5

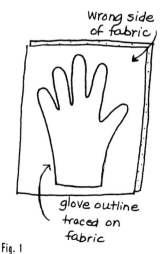

Wrong side of fabric

glove outline traced on fabric

Fig. 1

Reversible Headband

Use this headband to keep your hair away from your face during a facial or to keep your ears warm on a cold day. It's adjustable and reversible – a smart and stylish accessory adaptable for lots of uses.

Headbands can keep your ears warm or hold your hair away from your face for a facial. Helen and Naomi show both a cotton Lycra fabric headband and a Polarfleece headband. Both are reversible. Polarfleece by Malden Mills.

Supply List:
1/8 yd. fabric or two fabrics
for reversible feature
3" strip Velcro, 3/4" wide

1. On the tissue pattern sheets, locate the piece for the Reversible Headband. Place the pattern on the foldlines of two pieces of fabric and cut.

2. Try the fabric pieces around your head to test the length and overlap. Shorten the bands from both short ends, if necessary.

3. Sew Velcro at one end of each headband on the right side of the fabric. Place the pieces 1" from the ends. (Fig. 1)

Velcro sewn on 1" from band end

right sides of both fabrics

Fig. 1

4. To add a hanging loop on the headband (see the photo on page 71), cut a strip of fabric 3" x 1". Turn under one 3" edge and fold the other 3" edge into the center to form a narrow strip. Sew down the center. Pin the strip in a loop at one end of the headband without Velcro. (Fig. 2)

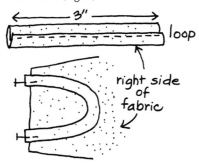

3"

loop

right side of fabric

Fig. 2

5. Place the two headband pieces with right sides together and with the Velcro sections at opposite ends. (Fig. 3)

Velcro

Wrong side of fabric

Fig. 3

Sew around three sides of the bands with 1/4" seam allowances, leaving the end without the loop open for turning. (Fig. 4)

Wrong side of fabric

open

Fig. 4

Trim the seam allowances and pull the headband right side out through the opening at the end. Press the edges. If you've made the headband from Polarfleece, lightly bounce the steam iron over the seamlines to flatten but not smash the fabric.

6. Turn under the raw edges of the open end and topstitch closed. Continue topstitching around the entire headband. (Fig. 5)

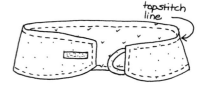

topstitch line

Fig. 5

Options:

* Make the headband from terrycloth or other absorbent fabric for use during exercising. I used ribbing fabric as one side of the spa headband; it's a knit and stretch fabric like the Lycra fabric used in my spa accessories.

This headband is quick to sew and makes an excellent addition to the spa accessory collection. To store the accessories, sew a Pleated Pouch (page 86) and add Lycra trim on each side of the zipper. This is a wonderful gift package.

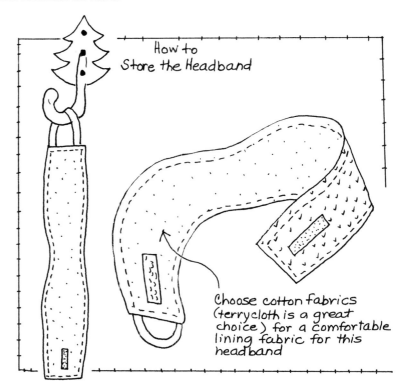

How to Store the Headband

Choose cotton fabrics (terrycloth is a great choice) for a comfortable lining fabric for this headband

Pocket Necklace

Wear this necklace as a piece of jewelry, a holder for credit cards, hotel room keys, or money... you decide. Both sides are decorated with machine applique but many other embellishment ideas can be chosen for the necklace trim. The length of the necklace is adjustable so it can complement a variety of outfits. One side of the black necklace is shown on the book's front cover. The other side is pictured here.

The large rock in my viola flower patch is a perfect table for three pocket necklaces. The black necklace features appliques included in this book; the applique on the other side of the necklace is shown on the book's front cover. In the center, the tan linen necklace shows an applique/embroidery design I created for Husqvarna Viking embroidery sewing machines. The third necklace is sewn from a brown Hoffman batik, with a patch of rubber stamping accented with gold beads. This necklace style is fashionable and functional as the open pocket top accommodates credit cards or hotel room key cards and even a little money. Rubber stamp by All Night Media, necklace cording and tassels by Wrights.

Supply List:

1/8 yd. fabric
scraps of fabric for applique
2 yds. 3/16" cording
1/2 yd. cord for beaded fringe
assorted beads and small tassels
5" x 12" piece of stabilizer
small pieces of paper-backed fusible web
bodkin for threading necklace cords
cellophane tape
Fray Check or clear-drying glue

1. Cut two pieces of fabric 5" x 6" for the front and back of the necklace. Also cut two pieces 1-1/2" x 4" for the side casings and two pieces 3-1/2" x 4-3/4" for the necklace pocket lining.
2. On the front and back fabrics, sew the applique designs shown on the necklace, or use two machine embroidery pieces from your embroidery stash. The entire applique designs are on page 78, but in trimming the fabric to cut the actual necklace front and back, parts of the designs were trimmed away. Use stabilizer under the fabric while stitching and then tear it away and press the designs. Cut the pieces down to 3-1/2" x 4-3/4" for the front and back. I found it helpful to cut a template from translucent plastic so I could move it over each design and select the best way to cut the fabrics. (Fig. 1)

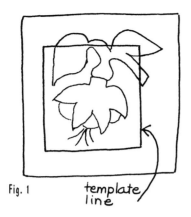

Fig. 1

template line

3. Fuse narrow strips of paper-backed fusible web on the narrow ends of the wrong side of the side casing fabrics. Peel off the paper and turn under 1/4" of the short fabric edges to the wrong side of the fabric and fuse. Press the casings in half with the wrong sides together. (Fig. 2)

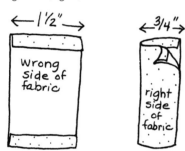

← 1 1/2" →

Wrong side of fabric

← 3/4" →

right side of fabric

Fig. 2

Pin to meet the raw edges of the necklace front, centering the casings on the sides of the front. (Fig. 3)

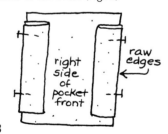

right side of pocket front

raw edges

Fig. 3

4. Add the fringe and tassels at the bottom edge of the necklace at this time. Cut cording strips 3" long and arrange them at the bottom edge, with the fringe extending on top of the necklace front. Tape the cords in place 1/2" from the bottom edge. (Fig. 4)

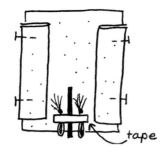

Fig. 4

tape

Now baste the casings and cords in place with a narrow seam allowance - less than 1/4". Reinforce the stitching over the cords.

5. Place the necklace back over the front with the right sides facing. Pin the sides and bottom edges together and carefully sew with 1/4" seam allowances. Sew from the side with basting stitches. Turn the pocket right side out to check that the casings and fringe are all sewn in place correctly and then restitch the sides and bottom edges for a strong seam. Clip and trim the seam allowances with pinking shears. Press. Turn right side out, remove the tape, push out the corners, and press again.

6. Sew the two lining pieces together with 1/4" seams along the 4-3/4" edges. Trim the seam allowances. Slide the necklace front and back piece inside the lining section and meet the raw edges. (Fig. 5)

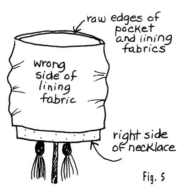

raw edges of pocket and lining fabrics

wrong side of lining fabric

right side of necklace

Fig. 5

Place the side seams of the lining fabrics away from the side seams of the front and back piece to avoid bulky corners on the pocket opening. Pin the edges together and sew with a 1/4" seam allowance, stitching on the inside

on the front and back fabrics. (Fig. 6)

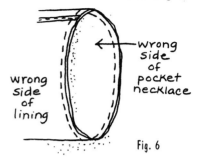

wrong side of lining

wrong side of pocket necklace

Fig. 6

Trim the seam allowances. Press, turn right side out, and press the seam again.

7. To close the lining, sew across the bottom 1/4" from the edge. Trim the seam allowances and insert the lining into the pocket. Press again.

8. String beads onto the cords sewn to the bottom of the necklace. Knot the cords to hold the beads in place. Add a little glue or Fray Check to keep the knots tied, especially on slippery cords.

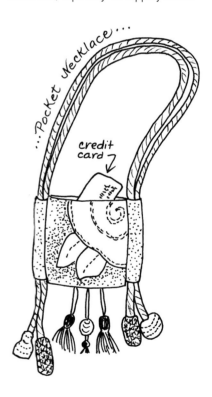

...Pocket Necklace...

credit card

9. Cut the 3/16" cord into two 36" pieces. Tightly tape the ends to prevent fraying and to make it easy to slide through the casing and to add beads. Attach a bodkin to the cords and slide them each through both casings on the sides of the necklace. This will be a tight fit but also makes the necklace length adjustable. (Fig. 7)

Fig. 7

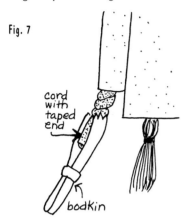

cord with taped end

bodkin

Slide beads on the cord ends, remove the tape, and knot the cord ends to keep the beads in place.

Options:
* Make this necklace without the pocket opening. The beige linen necklace shown features designs I created on card #27 for Husqvarna Viking machines. The finished necklace is 3-1/2" square and has one layer of thin quilt batting inside.

Can you see possibilities for this project? Look over your collection of special small pieces of fabric or embroidery designs that are especially beautiful. Won't they look great as a necklace?

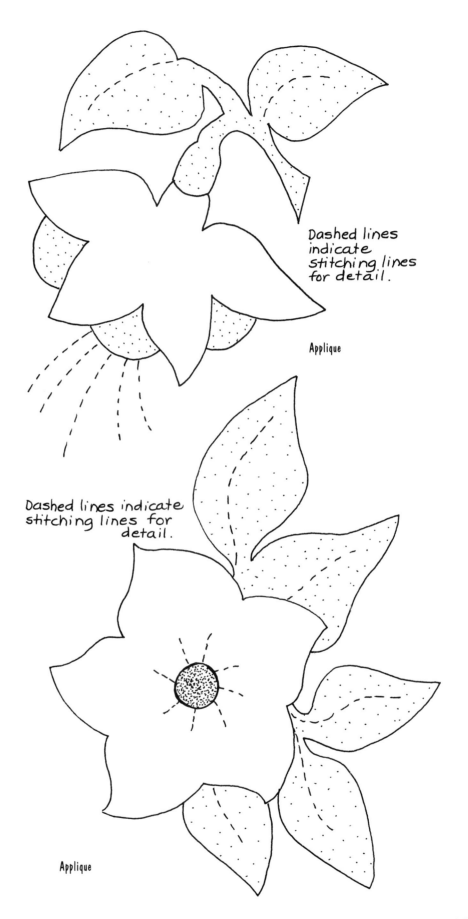

Dashed lines indicate stitching lines for detail.

Applique

Dashed lines indicate stitching lines for detail.

Applique

Movable Pockets

Like pockets? Do you wish every garment had pockets? Now it's possible when you make your own pockets to button on and move from jacket to skirt to dress to vest. This project was invented when a favorite jacket of mine didn't have a pocket. I appreciate having a small storage place on my clothing and sometimes it takes the place of a purse. Three versions are shown here, but they're just the beginning of possibilities. Here's a little secret I discovered: Use shank buttons and pin them on the garment and then your pockets can be moved and removed anywhere and anytime.

No pockets where you want pockets? Make movable ones. The denim/indigo pocket on the left has an open pocket on the front, a zipper pocket, and a combination of denim fabrics. The top edge is a strip of Ultrasuede with three openings for buttonholes. In the center, the flared-edge pocket features a Hoffman batik print and an open top pocket. Fabric loops hold the pocket to the buttons on the skirt waistband. The black and white pocket has three buttonhole tabs - and three different buttons - to hold it to the garment. The decorative zipper trim is made by Wrights and a rubber stamped design from an All Night Media stamp trims the open pocket section. Buttons by JHB International.

1. Select a garment or garments for pocket placement. Then select pocket fabrics to blend in or stand out. Also think about where the pocket will be buttoned to the garment. Are you left-handed? Then you'll appreciate having the pocket pinned on your left side.

2. Decide on the pocket size and shape. Use the patterns on the tissue sheets or make your own. Remember that there are no rules here for straight edges or regular shapes. Be creative and design your own shapes and make paper patterns of them.

3. Cut two of the main pocket shape from fabric. For any extra open pockets, cut an extra shape.

Denim/Indigo Pocket

1. Find the rectangular Movable Pocket pattern and cut two from fabric. Sew a zipper to the right side of one pocket piece 1-1/4" below the top straight edge, sewing around all four sides of the zipper. Cut away the fabric within the

stitching lines on the back of the fabric to expose the zipper teeth. Cut off any extra lengths of zipper on the ends. Sew pieces of ribbon or decorative braid over the edges of the zipper if you don't want the entire zipper to be exposed.

2. The extra open pocket on the lower portion of the denim/indigo pocket has a "V" edge. Using the tissue pattern, cut an extra facing about 1-1/2" wide. Sew the facing to the edge, trim the seam, and turn right sides out to make a neat edge for the pocket. Topstitch through the facing. (Fig. 1)

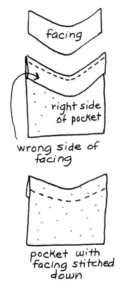

Fig. 1

Pin and sew the open pocket to the main pocket piece with the zipper already attached, meeting the wrong side of the "V" pocket to the right side of the main pocket. Cut a 6" x 1-1/2" strip of Ultrasuede for the buttonhole section of this pocket. Sew it to the top edge of the pocket front with the right side of the fabrics facing.

3. Open the zipper a short distance and place the pocket back fabric over the pocket front with the right sides together. Pin and sew all the way around with a 1/4" seam allowance. Trim and clip the seam allowances, press, and turn right side out through the zipper opening. Cut the button-holes in the Ultrasuede, making sure they are big enough for the buttons but not too big. (Fig. 2)

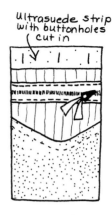

Fig. 2

Position the pocket on the garment and mark the spots for the buttons through the buttonhole openings. Sew or pin the buttons to the garment and button on the movable pocket.

Flared-Edge Pocket

1. For the flared-edge pocket on the skirt, cut three pocket fabrics using the Movable Pocket tissue pattern. Turn down 1", press, and sew across the top edge of one of the three pieces. Sew this piece, wrong side down, to the right side of one of the other two pieces. (Fig. 3)

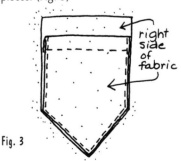

Fig. 3

2. Make loops for two buttons by cutting a 7" x 1" fabric strip. Turn under 1/4" and press both 7" edges. Fold one of these long edges to overlap the other and press again. Sew along the strip, near the top fold. Cut the 7" strip in two pieces. Fold each one in half and pin the ends to the right side of the larger pocket piece along the top edge. Sew across the ends a few times to secure them to the pocket. (Fig. 4)

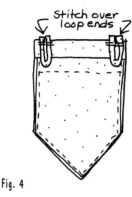

Fig. 4

3. Match and pin the third pocket piece with its right side over the right side of the larger pocket piece. Sew around the edges with a 1/4" seam allowance and leave an opening at the top edge between the loops. Trim the seam allowances and corners, press, turn right side out, and press again to flatten the pocket. Topstitch across the top edge of the pocket. Button it onto a skirt or other garment.

Black & White Pocket

1. For the black and white pocket shown on the jacket, use the Flared Movable Pocket pattern. Cut three pocket shapes from fabric.

2. Sew the zipper on an angle to the pocket front piece using the method given in Step 1 of the Denim Pocket. Cut away the fabric behind the zipper area. Sew the trim over the zipper edges. On the fabric chosen for the loose outside pocket, cut away the section that would cover the zipper area. (Fig. 5)

Fig. 5

Turn under and sew the edge to run parallel to the zipper or sew in piping as I did. Also trim the pocket, using buttons, machine embroidery, or a small sample of rubber stamping like the one I chose.

3. Cut a 6" x 2-1/2" piece of fabric for the buttonhole tabs. Sew the 6" edges together with right sides facing and then stitch across the strip at 2" intervals to divide the strip in three. Cut apart above the crosswise stitching. (Fig. 6)

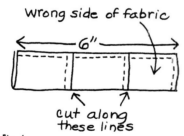

Fig. 6

Turn all three pieces right side out. Sew a vertical buttonhole near the finished end of each of the three tabs.

4. Pin and sew the tabs and open pocket (wrong side down) to the right side of the larger pocket front piece using a 1/8" seam. (Fig. 7)

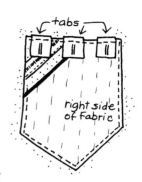

Fig. 7

Open the zipper. Pin the pocket back piece with the right sides meeting the pocket front. Sew around all the edges with a 1/4" seam allowance and reinforce the stitching across the tabs and at the edges of the open front pocket. Trim the seam allowances, press, turn right side out through the open zipper, and press again.

Options:
* Pin the pockets inside a garment if you want to hide valuable belongings - things like passports or credit cards.
* Use machine embroidery or pieces of vintage linens as trim or as portions of pockets or trim them with beads and buttons, tassels, or fusible bias tape... I could go on and on.

I hope you see endless choices for movable pockets. Remember that shank buttons are great to pin on the garment. Then, if you change your mind, you simply unpin the buttons.

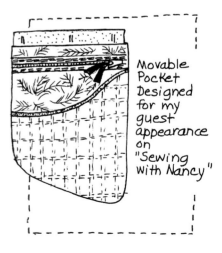

Movable Pocket Designed for my guest appearance on "Sewing with Nancy"

Checkbook Cover With Pen Holder

Do you spend time digging in the bottom of your purse for a pen each time you write a check? This checkbook cover can solve that problem for you and give your checkbook a stylish look as well.

Make your checkbook extraordinary with a new cover and the added feature of a pen holder. I chose Ultrasuede for this project because it's durable and easy to launder. You'll see my Coin Holder Key Ring under the checkbook, and also the red American Tourister vanity case I recently found at an antique shop. It's the style of suitcase every high school girl coveted back in the '60s. I didn't get one then, but now my dream has come true!

Supply List:

10" x 14" piece of Ultrasuede

small pieces of Ultrasuede for "checks" applique and pen holder tab

small pieces of paper-backed fusible web (Heat 'n Bond Lite Iron-On Adhesive is recommended)

small piece of stabilizer for applique area

2" strip Velcro, 3/4" wide, cut in half lengthwise

press cloth

1. Cut three pieces of Ultrasuede:
> 10" x 7"
> 7" x 3"
> 2-1/2" square for the tab

2. Begin by adding the applique shown below or a monogram (see the alphabet on page 93). Trace the design or letters on paper-backed fusible web. Fuse the design on the wrong side of the applique fabric. Cut with your sharpest embroidery scissors. *Hint:* Use a razor blade or craft knife to make a tiny slash cut in each area to be cut out, then use the scissors to trim out the area. Place and sew the applique(s) 1-1/2" above one end of the 10" x 7" piece of Ultrasuede. (Fig. 1)

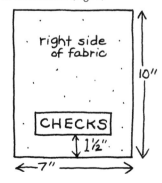

Fig. 1

right side of fabric · CHECKS · 1½" · 10" · 7"

Use a press cloth to fuse the design to the Ultrasuede fabric. Place a piece of stabilizer on the wrong side of the Ultrasuede beneath the stitching area. You can sew around each of the letters if you want to, but sewing with a straight stitch around the border of the design is adequate. Remove the stabilizer after stitching.

3. For sewing on Ultrasuede, you may find that a Teflon presser foot helps move the fabric smoothly as you sew. Sew a narrow strip of the loop (soft) side of Velcro to the center of the checkbook front. Place it 1/2" below the bottom edge of the applique, or 3/4" from the edge of the fabric. Pin the edge of the tab fabric to the edge of the checkbook fabric, with the right side of the tab facing up. (Fig. 2)

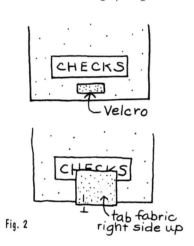

Fig. 2

4. On the opposite end of the checkbook fabric, turn up the end 3" with the right sides of the fabric together. (Fig. 3)

Fig. 3

Pin and sew down the sides of this flap, using a 1/4" seam allowance. Turn the pocket right side out and press with a press cloth.

5. Place the 7" x 3" fabric over the design area on the cover, with the right sides of the fabric facing. Use lots of pins to hold the two fabrics together and sew around the three sides with 1/4" seam allowances. Reinforce the stitching over the tab. Before turning the fabric right side out, stitch down the 1/4" seam allowances between the two end pockets of the cover. (Fig. 4)

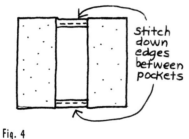

Fig. 4

6. Turn the pocket right side out and press, again with the press cloth over the fabric. Experiment with pens of different sizes in the pen holder. Plan where the hook side of the Velcro will be sewn and trim off the excess. Topstitch to attach the Velcro to the tab. (Fig. 5)

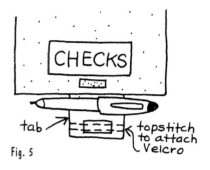

Fig. 5

Add the checkbook and register, a pen, and you're ready to experience more efficient, less frustrating check writing.

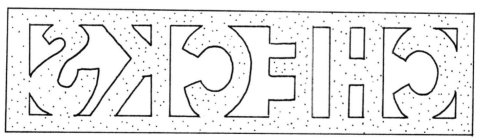

This applique design is printed backwards for ease in tracing onto paper-backed fusible web. Cut out white areas between letters after fusing design to applique fabric.

Potholder & Placemat Supply Holders

With a potholder, some zip-top plastic bags, a button, your sewing machine, and 15 minutes, you can make this handy holder for sewing supplies, crochet hooks, pens, first aid supplies, jewelry, embroidery floss, or office supplies. The placemat version holds a stationery collection, counted cross stitch projects, or makeup. Make one for a child with supplies for entertainment on a car trip: colored pencils, a tablet, stickers, scissors, paper dolls, a small color book.

Zip-top plastic bags sewn to a potholder or placemat turn these easy-to-find kitchen accessories into clever bags and supply holders. The potholder version holds writing and mailing supplies and the plaid placemat bag, with its larger gallon size zip-top bag, accommodates larger supplies and works great as a child's activity bag for car trips. The sunflowers are from my garden.

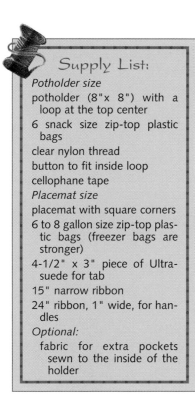

1. In the center of the wrong side of the potholder or placemat, draw a line parallel to the edge with the loop. (Fig. 1) Make sure the line will be easy to see even through the layers of bags on top.

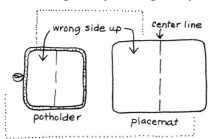

Fig. 1

2. Sew extra fabric pockets to the potholder or placemat, if you want them. (Fig. 2)

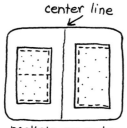

Fig. 2

3. Overlap the bottoms of six zip-top bags over the center line. Begin by taping the edge of the first bag to the potholder. Next, place and tape the second bag with its opening edge opposite the first bag. Alternate the bags and tape them in this way. (Fig. 3)

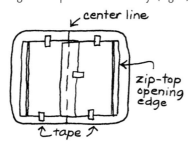

Fig. 3

4. Sew the bags to the potholder or placemat, stitching along the center line. Sew at least two lines to secure the bags. You can trim away some of the extra overlap of the bags. Sew the strip of narrow ribbon over the seams on the placemat version.

5. Sew the button to the right side of the potholder to line up with the loop on the opposite side of the potholder. (Fig. 4)

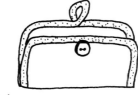

Fig. 4

6. For a tab closure on the placemat, sew one 3" end of the Ultrasuede piece to the back of the placemat. Cut a buttonhole into the opposite end of the tab. Sew or pin a button to the front of the bag. (Fig. 5)

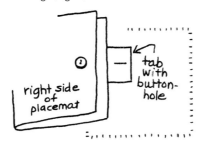

Fig. 5

7. Cut the 24" piece of ribbon in two 12" pieces. Fold the ribbon in half lengthwise. Stitch along the edges and leave 1-1/2" unsewn on each end. Turn under the ends of each handle 1/4". (Fig. 6)

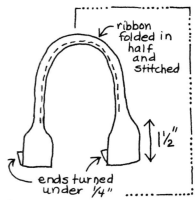

Fig. 6

Pin the ends onto the placemat 4" from each side and stitch in a square to anchor them. (Fig. 7)

Fig. 7

Options:

* Sew smaller size zip-top bags in addition to the large ones, for storing smaller supplies, such as stamps in a stationery holder.

* Sew divisions in the zip-top bags, keeping the stitching out of the zipper closings of the bags.

Now fill the bags with your supplies. Make a few more for gifts. Children like these bags as well as adults.

Pleated Pouches

Select fabrics from your stash for these clever bags. Pleats sewn into the fabric give the bags their interesting shape and dimensions.

The Pleated Pouches start out as a flat piece of fabric and the pleats formed and sewn on the sides give the bags an interesting shape. The light blue bag on the left features decorative braid trim and stitching on the sides of the zippers. The edges of the Ultrasuede bag in the center are bound with red bias tape. On the right, the quilted print bag has its edges near the zipper wrapped with ribbon and a yarn tassel serves as a zipper pull. The light blue fabric is by Dan River, and the ribbon is by C.M. Offray.

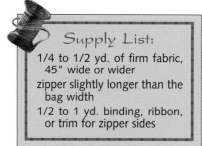

Supply List:

1/4 to 1/2 yd. of firm fabric, 45" wide or wider

zipper slightly longer than the bag width

1/2 to 1 yd. binding, ribbon, or trim for zipper sides

1. Make these bags any size you need. Here are the fabric sizes and zipper lengths for the bags pictured:

Light blue bag: 10" x 16" fabric, 12" zipper

Medium blue Ultrasuede bag: 12" x 14" fabric, 14" zipper

Navy print bag: 8″ x 12″ fabric, 9″ zipper

2. The first step for this bag is to add the binding or trim to the top edges of the fabric where the zipper will be sewn. If using ribbon or binding, press it in half, tuck in the cut fabric edge, pin, and sew. If using flat trim, sew the edging over the raw fabric edge on the right side of the fabric. (Fig. 1) You can also simply turn under and press the raw edges of the fabric if you do not want to add trim.

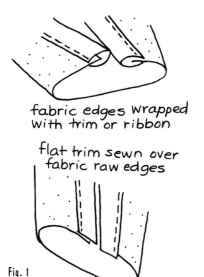

fabric edges wrapped with trim or ribbon

flat trim sewn over fabric raw edges

Fig. 1

3. Pin the zipper to the fabric edges you just sewed. Selecting a zipper longer than the bag width will make it easier to sew it in place. Sew the zipper to the trimmed edges, either with the zipper open or closed. Sew across the zipper ends. (Fig. 2) Cut off the extra length of zipper beyond the seams.

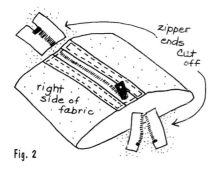

zipper ends cut off

right side of fabric

Fig. 2

4. Pin the folded pieces of ribbon over the zipper ends either as a tab or a loop. (Fig. 3)

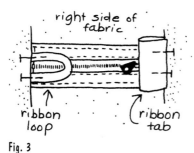

right side of fabric

ribbon loop

ribbon tab

Fig. 3

Fold the fabric with the zipper on one fold. Mark the fold line on the opposite side. (Fig. 4)

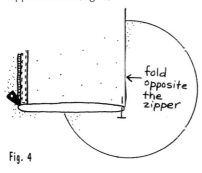

fold opposite the zipper

Fig. 4

Turn the bag wrong side out. Pin the center of the zipper end to the fold-line. Form pleats by tucking the fabric to meet the edges of the zipper trim. (Fig. 5)

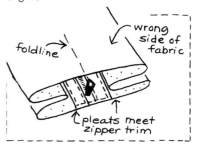

wrong side of fabric

foldline

pleats meet zipper trim

Fig. 5

5. Pin and sew across each bag end. Reinforce the stitching by sewing back and forth. Sew slowly through all the layers of fabric, ribbon, and zippers. (Fig. 6) For a finished edge, wrap and sew bias binding across the seamline.

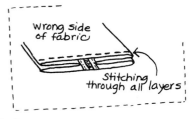

wrong side of fabric

Stitching through all layers

Fig. 6

6. Turn the bag right side out and push out the bag ends. Add a zipper pull of ribbon, Ultrasuede, or a yarn tassel.

See another of these bags on page 71 with the spa accessories. Notice the added monogram. Try a denim bag cut from old jeans. You can also line the bag with vinyl or cotton. This is just a beginning of the choices and options for these useful clever pouches.

Coin Holder Key Ring

With small pieces of fabric, you can create wonderful key rings that feature a storage pocket for coins, more keys, bandages, pills, or treasures.

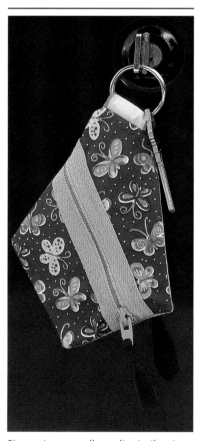

Store coins or small supplies in the zipper pocket of this key ring. Brightly colored fabrics make this key ring easy to spot in a backpack or purse. Fabrics by P & B Fabrics, ribbon by C.M. Offray.

Supply List:

small pieces of fabric for back and front of coin holder

small pieces of crisp interfacing

clear thread

zipper, 4" or longer

2-1/2" piece of ribbon, 3/4" to 1" wide

key ring

ribbon or cord for zipper pull

1. On the tissue pattern sheets, locate the piece for the Coin Holder and cut two from fabric.

2. Fuse interfacing to the wrong sides of both pieces of fabric.

3. Plan the placement of the zipper. On the key ring pictured, the zipper crosses the fabric at an angle. Pin and sew the zipper to the top fabric only. (Fig. 1)

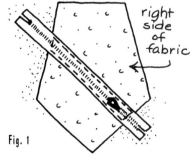

right side of fabric

Fig. 1

Sew two seams around the zipper and remember to pull the zipper head within the stitching lines. On the back of the fabric, cut away the fabric underneath the zipper teeth.

4. Fold the ribbon in half and pin the raw edges over the top narrow edge of the coin holder. Open the zipper a short distance. Pin the back fabric to the front with the right sides of the fabric meeting.

5. Sew with a short stitch length all around the coin holder, using 1/4" seam allowances. Trim the seam allowances close to the stitching lines and across the corners. Turn right side out through the zipper opening.

6. Press. Add a metal key ring to the ribbon and also tie on a zipper pull to make it easy to open and close the zipper.

Select colorful bright fabrics to make this coin holder key ring easy to find inside a purse. For coordinated accessories, make this key ring to match the checkbook cover project on page 82.

Decorating Ready-Made Accessories

Here are a few ideas for sprucing up the accessories you already have. There's nothing wrong with taking something purchased and trimming it to add a little more style. Here are some quick ideas to try.

Transformed Totes

Turn everyday totes into stylish bags with these ideas.

These used to be two ordinary tote bags. The red bag has an Anything Pocket made from a sewing print fabric by Hoffman and topped with a vinyl pocket for sewing supplies. The bag's original handles were replaced by pieces of vinyl tape measure by Prym Dritz. The denim bag is decorated with a photo of my sisters and me that was printed on colorfast printer fabric by June Tailor. My mother would have loved this bag.

1. On the red bag, I removed the original handles and replaced them with pieces cut from a plastic coated tape measure. On the bag front, a large Anything Pocket holds extra supplies and the vinyl pocket on top has piping around the edge. This is a perfect gift for a sewing friend.

2. The second tote bag is trimmed with a photo copied onto special colorfast printer fabric sheets. I used fusible bias tape to frame the edges of the photo and added a few buttons. This is a way to cover up a logo, stain, or just to trim a plain tote bag.

Plain tote bags are a perfect "blank canvas" for many decorations. I also like to use machine embroidery patches to trim the bags or to add as an outer pocket.

Polarfleece Pasta

The shape of bowtie pasta inspired this decoration. These fast and fun shapes are perfect small additions to gloves, purses, and headbands.

Use pinking shears and standard scissors to cut these simple shapes. Stitching them in pleats folded in the center creates the pasta look. Polarfleece by Malden Mills.

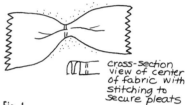

Supply List:
ready-made gloves (or make your own, see page 72)
Polarfleece scraps
pinking shears

1. Cut rectangles of Polarfleece 2" x 3-1/2" and cut the short edges with pinking shears.
2. In the center, pleat the fabric and sew across back and forth to hold the pleat in place. (Fig. 1)

Pin or sew the pasta on totes or wearable accessories.

Fig. 1

cross-section view of center of fabric with stitching to secure pleats

Lace-Trimmed Socks

Dress up a pair of ordinary socks with elegant lace. The socks should have a very stretchy top edge, stretching to at least 6" in width.

Add style to your legs and feet just by sewing lace to the tops of your stockings. Did you notice that I haven't identified the owners of the legs?

Supply List:
ready-made socks
12" to 14" of lace with an open bottom edge (see illustration)
thread to match socks

1. At the center back of the inside edge of the sock, begin zigzag stitching the lace to the sock edge. Stitch 5 to 6 stitches before you begin to stretch the sock. Stretch out 1" ahead of the stitching and sew and stop. Then

stretch another 1". Overlap the lace edges and zigzag the sides together.

When you wear the socks, turn down the top edge so the lace is hanging down, as you see in the photo.

Appliqued Scarves

Add appliques to plain scarves for an extra touch of class.

Appliques add style to scarves. The blue scarf is trimmed with applique/embroidery designs I created for use on Husqvarna Viking sewing machines. The white scarf in the center features the designs from my Cactus Punch design card "Appliques from Nature." The swirl design on the orange scarf is included on this page and on a design card I created for Amazing Designs.

Supply List:

ready-made scarf (or make your own, see pages 38 and 40)

scrap of thin fabric such as chiffon

KK2000 fusible spray

water-soluble stabilizer

thread to match both the applique and the scarf

Orange Scarf

1. Trace the applique shape and cut it from thin fabric, such as chiffon.

2. Spray the wrong side of the design with KK2000 and position the design on the scarf.

3. Pin water-soluble stabilizer to the wrong side of the scarf beneath the design. Match the top thread to the applique and the bobbin thread to the scarf. Use a new size 70 needle and set the applique stitch for a medium width (2.5 to 3.0) and a stitch length of .5 to .7. You may want to experiment before stitching on the scarf. Sew around the design shape and remove the stabilizer.

4. Press the scarf, using an iron set at the correct temperature.

Blue Scarf

1. The blue scarf is trimmed with appliques done on an embroidery sewing machine. Hoop two layers of water-soluble stabilizer. Use KK2000 spray on the wrong side of the scarf. Place the scarf inside the hoop on top of the stabilizer, patting the sprayed area to smooth it.

2. Select a design and thin fabric for the applique. Follow the steps of the applique procedure: outline stitching, removing the hoop to trim away close to the stitching, then reinstalling the hoop to continue satin stitching.

3. After the stitching is completed, remove the stabilizer from the hoop and wet the remaining stabilizer or tear it carefully away from the scarf.

White Scarf

1. The Polarfleece scarf features appliques stitched on the embroidery sewing machine without applique fabric! Again, use water-soluble stabilizer in the hoop and spray the scarf to position it within the hoop.

2. Stitch a design such as the ones shown on the scarf. Another option is to use solar-sensitive thread. Outdoors on a sunny day, this scarf will have more colorful designs than it has indoors.

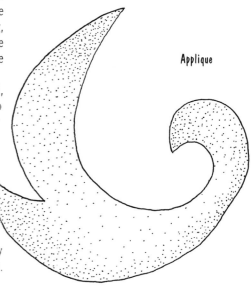

Applique

Polarfleece Blooms

Make a collection of flowers and leaves to trim a hat or other accessory. Use the patterns on this page for the blooms and leaves. Place the bloom pattern across the grain on Polarfleece. Cut all edges with pinking shears.

The brilliant tones of Polarfleece turn into striking flowers on this black hat Helen is wearing. She thinks this hat will brighten a cold winter day. Polarfleece by Malden Mills.

Supply List:

purchased hat
Polarfleece scraps
pinking shears

1. Cut the flower from Polarfleece using the pattern included. Gather the curved bottom edge of the flower with a long basting stitch. Pull on the threads to begin gathering. Wind one point of the fabric inside and sew it in place. You'll find the stitches will sink into the fleece and be invisible. (Fig. 1)

Continue to wind and gather the flower together. Bring the end point of the flower down toward the gathered edge and stitch in place. Knot and cut away the excess gathering threads. You have a small flower.

2. Cut leaves using the patterns provided. Cut the edges with pinking shears also. Pleat or gather the straight ends of the leaves and pin or sew them under the flowers.

3. Attach the flowers and leaves to your accessories with safety pins (a.k.a. silver and gold metallic fasteners, if you want to make them sound more elegant) or sew them in place.

secure one
end with
stitching

gathered
edge

Fig. 1

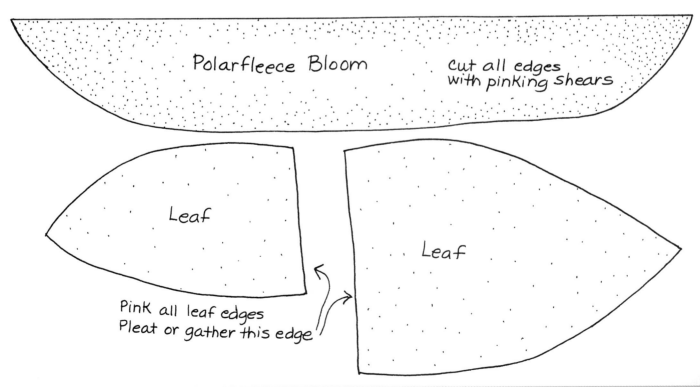

Polarfleece Bloom

Cut all edges
with pinking shears

Leaf

Leaf

Pink all leaf edges
Pleat or gather this edge

The Author Reports – August 2000

"How It Was When I Wrote This Book"

The idea for this book came to me while I was still finishing my last book, *Denim & Chambray with Style*. I started a list of projects but set it aside until I could concentrate on the topic before I proposed it to the editorial staff at Krause Publications.

The book idea was approved and a contract signed and then I began a series of seminar trips in the spring of 2000. I carried a notebook and whenever "accessory" thoughts came to me, I recorded them. From the positive response to the picture of me with my sisters in *Denim & Chambray*, I decided to feature my home in some of the photos of this book.

Then I began sewing in June. I spent the entire month with a tape measure draped around my neck and chained myself to my sewing parlour. (Sounds more elegant than just a sewing room, doesn't it?) The weather was rainy and days were dark, so I didn't feel like I'd missed summer. I started off putting away all my fabrics and sup-plies after each project so my work table was cleared off. It was a good idea. It's too bad I couldn't maintain the good habit. By the time I finished sewing, even the spare bedroom was a jumble of storage for my work. Periodically I'd show what I made to my sister Sarah, my friend Nancy, and Barry, my husband. Most of the time the response was enthusiastic. I brought projects to show when I spoke to the Lions Club, when I had dinner with Nancy's MinnTac Ladies, and when I attended the Two Judys' Brunch. It helps to get opinions and ideas, even from people who don't sew, and these outings gave me a break from solitary confinement in the sewing parlour.

During July I sat at the computer to compile the notes I had written after completing each project. The view from my window was lots of green lawn with young trees we've planted, one as a gift and memorial to my mother. I listened to Minnesota Public Radio and tapped away on the computer keys. I revised the manuscript, drew rough illustrations for the editors to see, and took pictures of my projects, also for the benefit of the editors.

Yet to come were the days of professional picture taking for the book, final manuscript revisions, final illustrations, and reading the galleys before the book goes to p[...]

It's always a thrill to se[...] for the first time, and page t[...] see how the pages turned out, but [...] just as exciting to hear from readers and to know your responses to what you find in my books and what you create as a result. Even if you haven't created anything yet, you are always welcome to send your thoughts and comments about my work and ideas. You can write to me at Box 87-K3, Aurora, MN 55705 (real mail is my favorite) or e-mail

mary@marymulari.com.

Here I am at work in the photo studio set up for this book... in my garage! Don Hoffman, the photographer, gets the credit for his very inventive photo ideas. The scenery outside of the camera lens is not arranged as neatly. See how the clothespins hold up the fabric background and the dressmaker dummies become catch-alls for the accessories already photographed.

Resources

...d Internet
...ducts fea-
...k with your
...pport them
...re as a busi-
ness co... ...ated for your
sewing needs.

Catalog of sewing supplies
Clotilde, Inc.
1-800-545-4002
www.clotilde.com

Catalog of sewing supplies, including Sensuede
Nancy's Notions
P.O. Box 683
Beaver Dam, WI 53916
www.nancysnotions.com

Buttons - manufacturer and wholesale source
JHB International
1955 S. Quince St.
Denver, CO 80231
www.buttons.com
e-mail for retail sources of JHB buttons:
sales@buttons.com

Sewing books, patterns, and embroidery cards
Mary Mulari
Mary's Productions
P.O. Box 87-K3
Aurora, MN 55705
www.marymulari.com
e-mail: mary@marymulari.com

Ultrasuede by the yard and piece
Michiko's Creations
P.O. Box 4313
Napa, CA 94558
www.suedeshop.com

Bug and other stencils, patterns by Diane Ericson
ReVisions
Box 7404
Carmel, CA 93921
www.revisions-ericson.com
e-mail: dericson@redshift.com

Polarfleece by Malden Mills
mail order source
1-877-289-7652
www.maldenmillsstore.com

Timtex hat brim fabric
Log Cabin Dry Goods
E3445 French Gulch Rd.
Coeru d'Alene, ID 83814
www.ior.com/~logcabin
e-mail: logcabin@ior.com

Patterns n' More
201 N. 8th - Suite B
St. Maries, ID 83861
www.patternsnmore.com
e-mail: patternsnmore@stmaries.com

Wholesale source for Timtex
Timber Lane Press
N22700 Rimrock Rd.
Hayden Lake, ID 83835
208-765-3353

Outdoor fabrics and supplies
The RainShed Inc.
707 N.W. 11th
Corvallis, OR 97330
541-753-8900
fax 541-757-1887

Yarns for embellishment and couching
Sally Houk Exclusives
50 Grand Boulevard
Shelby, OH 44875
419-347-7969

The Author Reports – August 2000

"How It Was When I Wrote This Book"

The idea for this book came to me while I was still finishing my last book, *Denim & Chambray with Style*. I started a list of projects but set it aside until I could concentrate on the topic before I proposed it to the editorial staff at Krause Publications.

The book idea was approved and a contract signed and then I began a series of seminar trips in the spring of 2000. I carried a notebook and whenever "accessory" thoughts came to me, I recorded them. From the positive response to the picture of me with my sisters in *Denim & Chambray*, I decided to feature my home in some of the photos of this book.

Then I began sewing in June. I spent the entire month with a tape measure draped around my neck and chained myself to my sewing parlour. (Sounds more elegant than just a sewing room, doesn't it?) The weather was rainy and days were dark, so I didn't feel like I'd missed summer. I started off putting away all my fabrics and sup- plies after each project so my work table was cleared off. It was a good idea. It's too bad I couldn't maintain the good habit. By the time I finished sewing, even the spare bedroom was a jumble of storage for my work. Period- ically I'd show what I made to my sister Sarah, my friend Nancy, and Barry, my husband. Most of the time the response was enthusiastic. I brought projects to show when I spoke to the Lions Club, when I had dinner with Nancy's MinnTac Ladies, and when I attended the Two Judys' Brunch. It helps to get opinions and ideas, even from people who don't sew, and these outings gave me a break from solitary confinement in the sewing parlour.

During July I sat at the computer to compile the notes I had written after completing each project. The view from my window was lots of green lawn with young trees we've planted, one as a gift and memorial to my mother. I lis- tened to Minnesota Public Radio and tapped away on the computer keys. I revised the manuscript, drew rough illustrations for the editors to see, and took pictures of my projects also for the benefit of the editors.

Yet to come were the days of pro- fessional picture taking for the book, final manuscript revisions, final illustra- tions, and reading the galleys before the book goes to print.

It's always a thrill to see a new book for the first time, and page through to see how the pages turned out, but it is just as exciting to hear from readers and to know your responses to what you find in my books and what you create as a result. Even if you haven't created anything yet, you are always welcome to send your thoughts and comments about my work and ideas. You can write to me at Box 87-K3, Aurora, MN 55705 (real mail is my favorite) or e-mail

mary@marymulari.com.

Here I am at work in the photo studio set up for this book... in my garage! Don Hoffman, the photographer, gets the credit for his very inventive photo ideas. The scenery outside of the camera lens is not arranged as neatly. See how the clothespins hold up the fabric background and the dressmaker dummies become catch-alls for the accessories already pho- tographed.

Resources

Check these mail order and Internet sources for some of the products featured in this book. Also check with your local sewing stores to support them and guarantee their future as a business conveniently located for your sewing needs.

Catalog of sewing supplies
Clotilde, Inc.
1-800-545-4002
www.clotilde.com

Catalog of sewing supplies, including Sensuede
Nancy's Notions
P.O. Box 683
Beaver Dam, WI 53916
www.nancysnotions.com

Buttons - manufacturer and wholesale source
JHB International
1955 S. Quince St.
Denver, CO 80231
www.buttons.com
e-mail for retail sources of JHB buttons:
sales@buttons.com

Sewing books, patterns, and embroidery cards
Mary Mulari
Mary's Productions
P.O. Box 87-K3
Aurora, MN 55705
www.marymulari.com
e-mail: mary@marymulari.com

Ultrasuede by the yard and piece
Michiko's Creations
P.O. Box 4313
Napa, CA 94558
www.suedeshop.com

Bug and other stencils, patterns by Diane Ericson
ReVisions
Box 7404
Carmel, CA 93921
www.revisions-ericson.com
e-mail: dericson@redshift.com

Polarfleece by Malden Mills
mail order source
1-877-289-7652
www.maldenmillsstore.com

Timtex hat brim fabric
Log Cabin Dry Goods
E3445 French Gulch Rd.
Coeru d'Alene, ID 83814
www.ior.com/~logcabin
e-mail: logcabin@ior.com

Patterns n' More
201 N. 8th - Suite B
St. Maries, ID 83861
www.patternsnmore.com
e-mail: patternsnmore@stmaries.com

Wholesale source for Timtex
Timber Lane Press
N22700 Rimrock Rd.
Hayden Lake, ID 83835
208-765-3353

Outdoor fabrics and supplies
The RainShed Inc.
707 N.W. 11th
Corvallis, OR 97330
541-753-8900
fax 541-757-1887

Yarns for embellishment and couching
Sally Houk Exclusives
50 Grand Boulevard
Shelby, OH 44875
419-347-7969